MW00826541

TIMARION

Byzantine Texts in Translation

ADVISORY BOARD

Harry J. Magoulias, General Editor
Barry Baldwin
John W. Barker
George T. Dennis
Emily Albu Hanawalt
Peter Topping

TIMARION

Translated with Introduction
and Commentary by

BARRY BALDWIN

WAYNE STATE UNIVERSITY PRESS
Detroit 1984

Copyright © 1984 by Wayne State University Press,
Detroit, Michigan 48202.
All rights are reserved.
No part of this book may be reproduced
without formal permission.

Library of Congress Cataloging in Publication Data

Timarion. English.
 Timarion.

 (Byzantine texts in translation)
 Bibliography: p.
 Includes index.
 I. Baldwin, Barry. II. Title. III. Series.
PA5385.T54E5   1984   883′.02   84-10426
ISBN 0-8143-1771-5

To Janet, Martha, and Alexander,
Who chorused,
Timarion who?

CONTENTS

PREFACE

I flatter myself that everything in the text is self-explanatory. By way of preface, it needs only to be mentioned for the benefit of readers and critics that my reading and bibliography takes account of work published up to the end of 1982. Only desultory notice could be taken of anything after that date.

I am most honoured by the invitation to translate the *Timarion* for the Wayne State University Press Byzantine Texts series extended by Bernard M. Goldman, director of the Press. I am also grateful to Professor Harry J. Magoulias, both for his help and encouragement and for the example his own translations of such Byzantine authors as Ducas and Choniates have set.

The necessary leisure for completion of this work was provided by the award of a resident research fellowship at the Humanities Institute of the University of Calgary. I am grateful to its director, Dr. Harold G. Coward, for this award and the facilities that came with it. I am also indebted to the other fellows (not Byzantinists or classicists) whose own interests and conversation were often helpful in clarifying the broader issues. Thanks are also due to my head of department, Dr. Martin Cropp, for permitting me to accept this fellowship at considerable inconvenience to the department at a time of budgetary restraint and staff shortages.

According to the dictates of brevity and intelligibility, titles of ancient works are given either in English or in the standard Latin form. Publication information of books cited is supplied in the Bibliography, as are titles of articles in journals or collections of papers.

INTRODUCTION

THE TEXT

The *Timarion* survives in a single manuscript, Codex Vaticanus graecus 87, datable to the fourteenth or early fifteenth century. In addition to extracts from Philostratus, Paulus Silentiarius, and the *Greek Anthology,* it also contains much of the work of Lucian. This, along with the style of the piece, is why the *Timarion* has traditionally been classified as pseudo-Lucian. It cannot, of course, be by Lucian, as it contains references to Byzantine individuals who lived many centuries later. Romano 39–40 gives an account of the manuscript and its history, along with references to other scholarly work, to which may now be added the discussion in J. Coenen's edition (Meisenheim, 1977) of Lucian's *Jupiter Tragoedus* (*Zeus Rants*). Through the courtesy of M. D. Macleod, Lucian's best modern editor, who pointed it out to me in a letter of February 14, 1982, I may add that although Romano abbreviates the manuscript to *V,* it is actually the Gothic *A* as described by Mras, Nilèn, and Macleod himself, who may include a text of the *Timarion* in the forthcoming volume 4 of his Oxford Classical Text of Lucian.

This manuscript was one of those brought to Paris around 1800 by Napoleon Bonaparte under the terms of the Treaty of Tolentino made with him by Pope Pius VI. One of Napoleon's *savants,* M. Hase, was deputed to make an inventory of these treasures from the Vatican library. The *Timarion* caught Hase's eye. He liked it and published it with Latin translation and notes in 1813. The German scholar A. Ellissen republished it at Leipzig in 1860, along with a text of the fifteenth-century satire *Mazaris,* which Hase had known of but had not edited. In 1974, R. Romano brought out the first modern edition, supplying the text used for the present translation. Should Macleod include the *Timarion* in his edition of Lucian (at the time of writing, this had not been finally decided), he tells me that it will differ from

Romano's only in the few small details signalled in his review in *JHS* 96 (1976), 271.

THE TRANSLATION

In making this first English translation, I have faced the usual problems of any translator and have adopted most of the usual solutions. Fidelity to the meaning of the original is naturally the first consideration. But this cannot always be readably achieved by sticking to every word and sequence of that original. Greek is a very different language from English in terms of structure and nuance, and this frequently compels the translator to addition and adaptation if he is to achieve a version that is both an accurate reflection of the original and a literate version thereof.

As befits a Byzantine imitation of Lucian, the *Timarion* flows along for much of the time in a fairly elegant and no-nonsense Greek that Atticises to a moderate and tolerable degree. However, as my notes disclose, there are some sequences, generally purple passages of description of someone or something, which are convoluted and occasionally difficult to the point of obscurity.

This is one reason why the tone of the translation is, perforce, not uniform. Another is the frequent insertion of quotations from and allusions to classical literature, a matter discussed below. A third is occasioned by the author's not always very successful attempts to give life to his protagonists Timarion and Kydion by having them engage in mutual banter and raillery for the first part of the dialogue. Here, some colloquial Greek is ventured upon, which always causes particular anguish to a translator, though mercifully the *Timarion* does not give him the problem of "four-letter words" or obscenity. I have made a special effort in these matters to achieve a neutral (mid-Atlantic, as it might nowadays be called) tone. George Bernard Shaw once said that England and America were two countries separated by the same language. As with much of what Shaw wrote, this is a partial truth expressed in extreme terms. Modern comedians can still get a laugh out of the different meanings of "knock up" in British and American English. With the hope that this translation may find readers on both sides of the Atlantic and the intent that neither side will be bothered by the esoteric slang of the other, I have avoided any distinctively British or American flavour. As a transplanted Englishman who has lived and taught in North America for nearly twenty years, I feel reasonably capable of success here. To this end, I have been particularly careful to avoid the use of sporting metaphors. Most North Americans do not play cricket, and most people in Britain know little about baseball; even a piece so relatively straightforward as the *Timarion* provides quite enough problems for the modern reader without needlessly giving him more.

It needs to be emphasised how I have tried to overcome the biggest of these problems. "Shakespeare," a student is supposed once to have asked, "isn't he the one who wrote the plays with all the quotations in them?" Byzantine authors liked to show off their erudition by stuffing their writings with quotations from and allusions to the Greek classics. They also aimed to flatter their readership by often leaving it to them to recognise this or that source for themselves. There is an excellent discussion of this in Hunger's *DOP* article listed in the Bibliography. The modern student is much more likely to be bothered than flattered by this habit. Hence, I have added such formulae as "in the words of Homer," "as Euripides says," and so on, which are not in the Greek text. Sometimes, to vary the diet when it is a particularly famous or hackneyed quotation, I have said (for instance), "in the words of the poet," just as we refer to Shakespeare as "the bard"; in these cases, however, I have added a formal reference in the notes.

THE COMMENTARY

Any commentary that tries to be all things to all people is liable to sink under the weight of excess baggage. Nevertheless, I have preferred to risk putting in too much rather than too little. After all, the individual reader can easily skip over what he does not want or need: better that than to leave him floundering. And as this is the first English edition, one cannot always cross-refer to predecessors. Some readers, of course, will understand, German, Italian, or Latin, and they have frequently been guided towards the commentaries of Ellisen, Hase, and Romano. But there is nothing else for the strictly anglophone.

I have assumed that my reader is intelligent, with a general knowledge of the more famous names of antiquity, someone who does not need to be told who Homer was or where Constantinople is. What he or she needs is basic, sometimes detailed, guidance on the history (in all its forms) of the period, as well as on the relevant contemporary literature and texts. Since Byzantine history and literature are often unfamiliar to the classical scholar, not to mention that elusive beast the general reader, I have not been too afraid of telling people what they already know.

Since the notes are designed to accompany a translation, not a Greek text, they do not go into points of grammar, except where these are relevant to the interpretation of a difficult passage or to explain my choice of reading where the text is in dispute. But I have devoted a considerable amount of attention to the language of the *Timarion,* at the risk of sometimes boring the Greekless reader. To provide some feel of the author's linguistic preferences, his liking or otherwise for inventing new words or reviving old ones, his overall vocabulary as compared to other Byzantine writers, seems an essential part of literary appreciation. An extra reason, as my subsequent discussion will show, is that scholarly arguments as to who the author of the *Timarion* may have been often turn on questions of vocabulary as well as content. Therefore, without at least some of the comparative evidence before him, the reader would not be able to follow these arguments, or see the basis for my own preferences. Finally, there are a few occasions where the Greek is difficult and more than one translation of a word or phrase possible. In these situations, I have set down the linguistic basis for my own judgements as fully as possible.

BYZANTINE SATIRE AND HUMOUR

What follows here is a brief survey of Byzantine satirical and other humour apart from the *Timarion,* designed both to provide the *Timarion* itself with a literary context and to encourage the reader to feel (and subsequently explore for himself) that the quality of Byzantine secular literature is sometimes a good deal higher than what is usually conceded. I here draw heavily on my recent paper, "A Talent to Abuse: Some Aspects of Byzantine Satire," *Byzantinische Forschungen* 8 (1982), 19–28. The reader should refer to this for more detailed and technical discussion of some points, and for references to primary sources along with bibliography of secondary literature. In the light of this, I eschew documentation in the following sketch, except for one or two parenthetical references where it is particularly useful to identify the source of a controversial remark or influential judgement.

The Byzantines are rarely accused of being great comedians. Indeed, they are rarely allowed any merit, artistic or otherwise. Nowadays, the very word Byzantine is exclusively a pejorative adjective, used to describe the hierarchies of political *apparatchiks* or the cloak and dagger manoeuverings of university administrators.

This usage was largely the invention of Montesquieu, one of many European writers who stigmatised the mediaeval Greek civilisation. For him, "the history of the Greek empire is nothing but a tissue of rebellions, sedition, and treachery."

Voltaire was far nastier: "There exists another history more ridiculous than the history of Rome after Tacitus; it is the history of Byzantium. This worthless collection contains nothing but declamations and miracles. It is a disgrace to the human mind."

Equally, Hegel: "The general aspect of Byzantium presents a disgusting picture of imbecility; wretched, even insane, passions stifle the growth of all that is noble in thoughts, deeds, and persons."

Finally, a Frenchman who himself made a lot of history once

5

urged his Assembly in a speech during the Hundred Days not to be like Byzantium and become a joke to posterity. Napoleon Bonaparte, obviously.

On the other side of the channel, all of these attitudes converge in Edward Gibbon, who practically invented the notion of Decline and Fall and who has imposed his vision of Byzantium on all subsequent generations of Englishmen. Having reached only the early seventh century in the first forty-seven chapters of his "damned thick great book"—as one contemporary called it—Gibbon suddenly accelerates and roars through the next five centuries in chapter 48. Clearly, he was eager to have done with what (to choose one of many quotable quotes) he characterises as "a tedious and uniform tale of weakness and misery. On the throne, in the camp, in the schools, we search, perhaps with fruitless diligence, the names and characters that deserve to be rescued from oblivion."

Now it is possible that these critics might have tempered their spleen, had they had access to the Byzantine literature we do. The one thing the modern student cannot complain about is shortage of material. Migne's *Patrologia Graeca* fills one hundred sixty-one volumes, each averaging two thousand pages or so. But up to Gibbon's time Byzantine texts were either theological, a genre for which he did not care, or historical ones (thanks largely to Louis XIV, under whose patronage they had begun to be printed in the Louvre series in Paris) which he read for facts rather than aesthetic pleasure. It is only since the nineteenth century that the riches of Byzantine secular literature began to be found, printed, and savoured. Much remains to be done, which is, of course, one of the chief attractions of being a Byzantinist.

Yet familiarity is said to breed contempt, and the increase in material has not automatically raised Byzantine standing on the scholarly hit parade. To continue in the best Byzantine manner with quotations from distinguished predecessors, I now parade the judgement of the late Romilly Jenkins (*Dionysius Solomos* [Cambridge, 1940], 57), who concluded that "the Byzantine Empire remains almost the unique example of a highly civilised state, lasting for more than a millennium, which produced hardly any educated writing which can be read with pleasure for its literary merit alone." A grim verdict, one endorsed by other experts, notably Cyril Mango in his Oxford inaugural lecture, "Byzantine Literature as a Distorting Mirror" (*PP* 80 [1975], 3–18), and widely disseminated by classicists who hold it as an article of faith that great Greek literature could not by definition be produced in a period in which *apo* governs the accusative case.

In the course of his paper on the Hellenistic origins of Byzantine literature (*DOP* 17 [1963], 39–52), Jenkins briefly touched on the issue of Byzantine humour but only in a single dismissive sentence: "Satire, indeed, was to some extent revived in later centuries; but it is satire that has lost all urbanity and charm."

This blinkered view was perhaps excusable in the old days. That it should have persisted in tandem with the opening up of the riches of Byzantine secular literature is a sad situation for those who know better and a misleading one (to say the least) for those who do not. By Jenkins' time, it was also an oddly regressive one. When H. F. Tozer brought out what was in his day a pioneering article on Byzantine satire (*JHS* 2 [1881], 233–70), he expounded good historical and human reasons for *assuming* the existence of a satirical tradition: "Repression, whether in the character of political despotism or of literary mannerism—and both of these existed in the Byzantine Empire—has the effect of forcing genius into side channels, and criticism, when it cannot be exercised openly, finds for itself indirect methods of expression, which are usually characterized by a tone of bitterness." Tozer knew from Hase's *Notices et extraits des manuscrits* of a dozen or so examples. But the student who turns to Baynes and Moss, *Byzantium: An Introduction to East Roman Civilisation* (Oxford, 1949), 239, will find only the *Philopatris, Timarion,* and *Mazaris* acknowledged, whilst the reader of Runciman's *Byzantine Civilisation* (London, 1933), 247, is given the same three titles and the flat statement "even satire was rare."

The *Timarion* and *Mazaris* are usually classified together as Lucianic. This is predictable but misleading. Paradoxically, the two pieces are both more and less Lucianic than their editors suggest. A comic descent to Hades inevitably reminds one of Lucian (equally, or so it should, of the *Frogs* of Aristophanes), but at least in the case of the *Mazaris,* given its fifteenth century date, may also comport parody of such romantic and serious literary descents as the *Apokopos (After Toil)* of Bergadis and the *Dirge on the Bitterness and Insatiability of Hades* of Johannes Pikatoros. Incidentally, those who seek to find both wit and universality in ancient literature should savour the fact that the plot of the *Timarion,* a man dying before his time and being restored to life, anticipates in large measure the popular movie *Heaven Can Wait.* In its turn, the *Timarion* gets the idea from Lucian's *Lover of Lies.*

The *Timarion* is at times a veritable cento of Lucianic phrases. The *Mazaris,* by contrast, is not: the only formal debt is a punning use of the *Lucius or the Ass* title. Needless to say, the author will have been familiar with Lucian. His satire was written at the time of the emperor Manuel II, whose correspondence (a letter to Chrysoloras quotes from *Zeuxis* 2) vouchsafes his own enthusiasm for Lucian. The *Mazaris* proper is postluded by three attachments: the narrator's resurrection dream and two letters. The form and purpose of these puzzle the most recent editors, leading them to speculation about sequels produced in response to the success of the main dialogue. In truth, it need be nothing more than imitation of Lucian's *Saturnalia,* where the main piece is followed by a group of mock letters.

De gustibus non est disputandum. So I shall simply disagree with Krumbacher's low opinion of the *Mazaris* ("Die Hadesfahrt des Mazaris ist zweifellos die schlechteste der bis jetzt bekannt gewordenen Imitationen des Lukian"), my own enthusiasm for its crude vigour being helped by sharing the author's fondness for paronomasia. In its largely contemporary content, it differs markedly from the safe, classicising universality of Lucian's targets. For a similar fourteenth-century exercise, one might compare Alexius Macrembolites and his

Dialogue between the Rich and Poor, on which, however,
I. Sevcenko (*Zbornik radova Vizantoloskog instituta* 6 [1970],
187–228) concluded that it is "not evidence of articulate revo-
lutionary thinking in Byzantium, a thing which in my opinion
did not exist." One feature may be singled out as having wider
and important application. A favourite theme of the *Mazaris* is
the iniquity of the medical profession. So also of the *Timarion,*
a detail stressed in Nigel Wilson's introduction to the extract
offered in his *Anthology of Byzantine Prose.* This is not a
Lucianic feature, Lucian himself generally showing marked respect for the profession. But it is a traditional theme of Greek
literature; witness the many epigrams in the *Greek Anthology,*
or Athenaeus' caustic remark (15. 666a), "Were it not for the
doctors, there would be nothing more stupid than the professors." Hence as will be discussed in detail later, one of Romano's arguments for Nicolas Callicles as the author of the
Timarion, turning on his medical expertise, is invalid.

"Lucianic" is also the epithet bestowed upon the prose satires of Theodore Prodromos. Here, again, we must discrimi-
nate. Self-evidently so is the *Sale of Lives,* though even here
notice the difference of sale objects between the two: philosophers in Lucian, men of letters and public life in Prodromos.
Not at all Lucianic is the *Executioner or Doctor,* which is one
of the most wincingly gripping comments on dentistry I have
ever come across. In selecting this target, Prodromos demon-
strates some originality. Dentistry does not even make the
indexes of Phillips' *Greek Medicine* or Scarborough's *Roman
Medicine.* From the technical writers, one can insert Celsus,
On Medicine 7. 21, an account of dental surgery that does
nothing to weaken the force of Prodromos' satire. In opting
for a medical theme (as he does elsewhere; cf. my note 87),
Prodromos is conditioned by two things beyond personal expe-
rience: literary tradition and the fear and hatred of doctors
manifested, most strikingly, in the Lives of the early Byzantine
saints.

"Fusion" is an operative word in considering Byzantine satire. The Third Beggar Poem (see my commentary for these)

inveighs against abbots who feast in the midst of their starving monks, a theme transplanted from classical literature, notably Juvenal's Fifth Satire. Prodromos' tragic parody *Battle of the Mice* certainly owes something to Lucian's *Goddess Gout;* both merit comparison with Housman's *Fragment of a Greek Tragedy*. The mock inscriptional decree of the kind found in the *Timarion* is another Lucianic device, one also employed in a satiric text published by Hunger with the enchanting title *Gegen eine byzantinische Mafia*. Parody of official language is the style of the *Porikilogos* and its imitation the *Opsarologos,* about fruit and fish respectively. These, along with various animal fables, may be placed in a loose tradition extending from (after Aesop and Phaedrus, of course) the fourth-century-Latin *Will of a Pig* to Orwell's *Animal Farm*. Obscenity is another satirical technique, one notably absent from the *Timarion*, evidenced in a mild way by the comic catechism *On the Whores* and very much more powerfully by the blasphemous *Office or Mass of a Beardless Man*. This latter is a rare piece of Byzantine profanity, perhaps implying some fourteenth- or fifteenth-century disillusion with the Church for letting down spiritual expectations. It is nicely characterised by D. M. Nicol, *Church and Society in the Last Centuries of Byzantium* (Cambridge, 1979), 100, as samizdat literature. The piece, comprising some eighteen hundred lines of verse and prose—a medley recalling the Menippan satire of Greece and Rome—has always been read and condemned for its (in Politis' words) outrageous obscenity which passes all bounds. "What rubbish, what filth, what blasphemy," wrote the humanist Martinus Crusius in his copy of the 1562 Venetian printed edition, and a glance at the other comments assembled in Eideneier's edition (Berlin, 1977) discloses a tradition of marginal abuse comparable to that afflicting Lucian. Alas, I like a good piece of earthy humour as much as the next, but the limited and endlessly repetitive invective of the work makes it the sort of thing that gives pornography a bad name.

As to the *On the Whores*—Bishop Marbodus wrote a poem in Latin in the eleventh century on the same subject, available in volume 171 of Migne's *Patrologia Latina*—insofar as Justinian and Theodora notoriously tried to get the girls off the streets and into the Convent of Repentance, a social reform emulated some centuries later by Michael IV (Psellus, *Chron.* 4. 36)—no doubt with equal lack of success—prostitution can be thought of as a real issue. But we need not take the word *pornas* ("whores") too seriously in the present context, much less should we suppose that the author is some sort of Byzantine tabloid reporter advocating a cleanup of the streets. The theme is simply part of the rich, classical tradition of misogyny, genuine or affected, that informs a great deal of Greek and Roman satire.

The abusive impulse was not, of course, unique to the Byzantines. It was part of their classical tradition, a point made very clear by Anna Comnena's use of the Latinism *phamousa* to describe the libellous pamphlets flung into her royal father's tent. Michael Jeffrey's classic study (*DOP* 28 [1974], 143–95) of the political verse correctly reaches back to the soldiers' songs and popular graffiti of imperial Rome recorded by Suetonius. A popular title or subtitle to Byzantine verse onslaughts is *Abusive Iambics,* denoting a tradition going back to Archilochus, although I know of no classical precedent for the emperor Theophilus' branding of metrically irregular (deliberately so, to aggravate the shame) verses onto the foreheads of two monks, an incident naturally not recalled in the *Timarion*'s kindly treatment of that emperor.

In his *Anatomy of Satire* (which largely ignores the Byzantine contribution), Gilbert Highet drew the following distinction: "Satire wounds and destroys individuals and groups in order to benefit society as a whole. Lampoon is the poisoner or the gunman. Satire is the physician or the policeman." There is something in that. Nevertheless, its real-life basis is certainly one reason why satire, unlike some other genres, was successfully pursued by the Byzantines. The abundance of material can be seen in Beck's *Geschichte der byzantinischen Volksliteratur.* The acclamations of the circus factions furnish one obvious example. John Lydus (*On the Magistrates* 3. 46) quotes some anonymous verses against the emperor Anastasius (491–518) placarded at the Hippodrome. A satirical inscription was affixed to the column of Justin II (565–78) by what John of Ephesus calls "some of the city wits." Byzantine humour, like that of any other civilisation, often depends upon the physical deficiencies of the target. An early example is the scene in Procopius, *Secret History* 15. 25–35, where Theodora has a group of eunuchs mock the hernia of a venerable patrician in a parody of church responsions. The history of Ducas (20. 6) provides a good final example of it. Sophia of Montferrat, imported from Italy by Manuel II to be the wife of his son John, had a superb figure and gorgeous blonde hair down to the ankles but was cursed with a most revolting face, which, in the historian's own words, caused her to be popularly described as "Lent from the front and Easter from behind."

The name of Lucian has kept cropping up, regarding whom a mistake has been made by those unfamiliar with Byzantine habits. Thanks to the vitriolic notice in the Byzantine encyclopaedia known as the *Suda* (formerly, Suidas) and the thirty-nine abusive epithets hurled at him by scholiasts, covering a wide range from atheist to paederast, Lucian acquired in some quarters the reputation of being the Anti-Christ. I have explored this issue more fully in "The Church Fathers and Lucian," *Studia Patristica,* vol. 18, ed. E. Livingstone (Oxford, 1982), 626–30. The present point is, he was no unique victim of this sort of abuse. Many of the same epithets are (predictably) flung at the emperor Julian. Collation of the word index in Westerink's Teubner edition of the *Scripta Minora* of Arethas (the scholarbishop who assailed Lucian as much as anyone) with the list of insults employed by Lucian's scholiasts shows that Arethas used at least a dozen of the same; and the satirist was not his only target. Nor was Arethas the only person to crack nuts with sledgehammers. Photius on John Philoponus, for instance, or on Lucius Charinus is just as brutal in his *Bibliotheca*. Or take John Tzetzes on practically anyone, calling as he does one victim "Bull-father, moonstruck son of a goat." Scurrillity was a tool of the Byzantine critical trade.

Some, but not all, of these ingredients are present in the

Timarion. It contains mockery of doctors, some abusive exchanges, and, if Constantine Acropolites (on whom, see later) is right, a blasphemous tone. On the other hand, misogyny is precluded by the absence of female characters, and there is no obscenity of word or content. In the *Mazaris,* by contrast, there is much crude talk, and women are referred to in terms of their supposed lewdness. The author of *Timarion* has clearly made his artistic choices, since both Byzantine practice and his Lucianic model permitted these features. To what extent he has succeeded in his satirical aims is naturally a matter for individual taste. Details will be discussed in the commentary. One purpose of the above survey was to show that the author is no unique, unexplained phenomenon, as might have been suspected by those brought up on a diet of the modern sneers at Byzantine literature quoted earlier. On the contrary, he was but one of many practitioners operating in a genre clearly as congenial to the Byzantines as to the modern world. The existence and popularity of satire does much to correct the prevailing image of the Byzantines and their society.

TO HELL AND BACK—BYZANTINE STYLE

After some hesitation as to its usefulness, I decided to include this précis of the *Timarion* on the grounds that it would serve both to clarify the position of the piece in the traditions of its genre, and to assemble some of my own views on its overall literary quality, views that are, of course, developed in the commentary but which might sometimes be obscured in the unavoidable thickets of information that notes must contain. To this end, the précis is presented in as brisk a style as possible, unencumbered by references of any kind.

The opening sections are by far the most boring. The narrator Timarion has returned behind schedule to Constantinople, where he is greeted by his old friend Kydion. This could and should have been kept to a brief *mise-en-scène* for the infernal travelogue to come. But the author is crippled by his very Byzantine need to show his readers how well he knows his classical models. Hence we have to endure endless repetition of the Lucianic opening gambit whereby Kydion, who is in modern terms only a boring feed to the narrator-star, keeps upbraiding his friend for being late home and for not giving him enough details about his adventures. During these opening exchanges the modern reader wants nothing so much as to shout at Kydion to shut up and let him get on with it. But that reaction is as futile as saying that Oedipus, given his destiny, should have avoided marriage and punching out strangers at traffic intersections. Even an author as refreshingly inventive as the writer of the *Timarion* could not escape the classical straightjacket. Nor, probably, did he want to, for the format allows him to show off his wide reading with a flurry of quotations from Homer and Euripides. Whether he had actually read the originals or merely got them from Lucian, who has some of the same ones, or from rhetorical handbooks is a moot point: any Byzantine could come up with a Homeric tag just as any of us know the quotable lines from *Hamlet.* Either way, the opening sequences resemble in their ostentatious learning nothing so much as a vintage Aldous Huxley novel.

When he is allowed to get down to brass tacks, Timarion discloses that the purpose of his outward journey was to go to the great northern Greek city of Thessalonica to attend the festival of its patron saint Demetrius held on October 26. His initial account affords interesting glimpses into how travel was organized in a large and dangerous world. Divine providence is constantly thanked for a safe journey, thereby playing more or less the role of a St Christopher medallion. Timarion travelled with an entourage of both his own and his father's friends. They stayed at friends' houses on the way rather than commercial establishments, though in Thessalonica itself and on the return we do find the party in lodging houses. They never get off the beaten track without first arranging that they will be met and escorted, and even on the main roads find reassurance in the sight of peasants working in the fields alongside. Altogether, a graphic reminder of the dangers of travel in mediaeval times. Later on in hell, the men guarding the entrance are compared physically to bandits who live in the mountains. It is, indeed, Timarion's eye for social details that make the work of such great interest, though it needs to be added that he is not uniformly practical. For he disingenuously reveals that he had taken no care to provision himself for the journey, being a student of philosophy.

Despite the rigours of earthly travel—it will later be seen that perambulation in hell is much easier—Timarion reaches his destination in good health and cheerful spirits. He had, no doubt by design, arrived before the day of the festival, which gives him that so-called modern problem, what to do with his leisure. On the one hand, he gloats over being on holiday from his studies. But, as he remarks with characteristic Byzantine anti-Semitism, idleness is to him as is pork to a Jew. Not that Timarion has any consistent philosophy on this. Later on, "pork butcher" is used as a term of abuse in a purely gentile context.

So Timarion and his companions go hunting, the sport of Byzantine kings at that time. Mercifully, we are spared macho tales of derring-do against dumb animals, though he would hardly have agreed with Oscar Wilde that hunting is a case of the unspeakable in pursuit of the uneatable. Instead, we get a florid description of where they went to hunt, namely the river Axios and surrounding countryside in Macedonia. The Byzantines were addicted to such *ecphraseis,* as they were called, of people, places, and things; the *Timarion* has many of them. As always, the author creates a linguistic pastiche from classical sources, achieving in this case a somewhat uneasy blend of Herodotus on the plain of Marathon and the *Hippolytus* of Euripides.

After more idiotic interruptions from Kydion, we get Timarion's description of the festival of Demetrius. It immediately receives the supreme Byzantine accolade: favourable comparison with the festivals of pagan Athens. But it is not simply a matter of religious celebration. Associated with the saint was a great fair, to which people flocked from as far afield as Italy, Spain, and France as well as from the region around.

Having spent much of my earlier life in Nottingham, England, I immediately think of that city's annual Goose Fair, allegedly more than six hundred years old, at which Arthur Seaton had some memorable moments in Alan Sillitoe's *Saturday Night and Sunday Morning*. The Thessalonica fair was one of many; these combinations of secular fair and religious festival persisted in Greece until the late nineteenth century, being adapted rather than abolished by the Turkish conquerors.

Timarion is one of nature's tourists. Nowadays, he would be boring us silly with colour slides of his last vacation. It was his first visit and, as he says in his prattling way, he was only a Cappadocian. So he went up to an overlooking hill, from which vantage point everything could be seen and described.

What follows is an elaborate *ecphrasis* of the aforementioned type, and is the section of the satire most commonly extracted for inclusion in textbook anthologies of Byzantine prose. Unluckily for students, it is also one of the hardest, being replete with rare or unparalleled words. Even though the author is one of the freshest commemorators of the social scene, he—to paraphrase Oscar Wilde—can resist everything except linguistic temptation.

Still, he achieves a vivid picture of the fairground with its many rows of merchants' booths, crisscrossing each other in parallel lines, with crowds jostling in the intervening aisles. He likens the overall effect to a giant centipede with very long belly and innumerable legs. Merchants were there from all parts of the world with goods of all sorts. It may be the eye of the Byzantine fashion commentator that makes him single out clothes of various kinds as the only detailed examples. It is not just the sights, but also the sounds, that impress Timarion. Taking the chance to use a phalanx of onomatopoeic verbs in the present participle, he describes the many animals, not so much there for sale as brought from home by their owners as protection against theft or wolves.

Having absorbed all this, Timarion returns to the city proper for the religious festival. This actually occupies three days and nights, with nocturnal hymn singing by choirs of clergy and monks presided over by the archbishop. Then, an *ecphrasis* of another sort. There is a daytime civil and military procession led by the local governor. The author takes the chance to describe the governor's pedigree, wife, family, and good looks in the most repulsively glowing of colours. As with several other characters in the satire, he is not directly named but is identified by clues in general and a laboured pun on his name in particular. Thus, mention of his old fame (*palaios logos*) at once alerts us to the presence of a member of the Palaeologus family that was destined to form the last dynasty in Byzantine history.

His beefcake physique and 8″ × 10″ glossy good looks are unremittingly described. The language becomes tortured and turgid, our author being at the mercy of literary convention as well as the demands of panegyric, not forgetting the baleful claims of physiognomy whereby a man's looks were confidently assumed to characterise his inner virtues. The only point worth singling out is the cultural confusion in which at one moment he is described in biblical quotation, at another in classical stereotypes. It is this very mingling of pagan and Christian elements, albeit not this particular passage, which earns the satire the aforementioned condemnation of Constantine Acropolites.

To the cheers of the crowd, this paragon of the virtues leads the invocation to St Demetrius, after which the lengthy hymn singing by antiphonal choirs of clergy and nuns is described. The ceremony complete, Timarion returns to his lodgings— apparently his father had no friends in Thessalonica on whom to sponge. It is at this point that the plot thickens.

Timarion fell ill. At first, it was the fever the ancients called tertian. Our narrator diagnosed this for himself, and went on a dreadful-sounding diet of vegetables and vinegar. Despite, or because of, this regimen, complications set in: his liver became inflamed, and violent vomiting and dysentery accompanied this. Timarion describes his various excretions in all-too-candid terms. But there is a reason for his grossness. His descent into hell and chances of return all hinge on the question of whether or not he had vomited up all his bile or not and was thus bereft of one of the four vital elements.

In spite of his condition, Timarion decided to try and get back to Constantinople. He had to be strapped across a pack horse like a parcel. Unsurprisingly, this exacerbated his condition, and when he reached the river Hebrus in Thrace, he had to stop and rest in lodgings. This is where the gothic horror begins.

It is midnight, of course. Everyone else is asleep. Timarion is tossing restlessly when suddenly two black devils come flying through the window and alight on his bed. Timarion is understandably paralysed with terror but is not too far gone to notice a piquant detail: the apparitions look travel-stained.

This is in fact a diabolical housecall, for the curious couple begin a loud medical conference to each other, speaking across the patient as though he were hardly there. They assert that a decree jointly posted in Hades by the old god of healing Aesculapius and the famous Greek doctor Hippocrates states that any person who has lost one of his four elements may not live longer. Turning now to the still speechless Timarion, they inform him that he is in this category and must join the fellowship of the dead.

Seizing the unresisting Timarion, the devils whirl him away through the air. They whizzed like arrows, observes the narrator, still sufficiently *compos mentis* to wax poetic and use some unique Greek adjectives to describe his flight. Zooming over the Acherusian Lake, one of several pagan details attached to his Christian vision, they come down at the edge of a deep pit, full of darkness, the pit of hell.

One of the devils plunges down it headfirst. Timarion now belatedly begins to struggle, but is pushed and punched down it.

Once at the bottom, they reach the entrance gate to Hades. This takes the form of a huge iron gate guarded by fiery dragons and that canine relic from the classical Hades, Cerberus. Cerberus seems somewhat tamed now, fawning on the devils and not requiring to be fed by sops. By contrast, in the most famous of all pagan-Christian infernal jumbles, Dante's *Divine Comedy,* he still (*Inf.* 6. 13) has to be bought off by sops.

This is a convenient moment to mention that there are several interesting points of similarity between Dante and the *Timarion*. One or two will be spotlighted later. There are also interesting differences. Charon and his ferryboat makes no appearance in the *Timarion*. But Dante (*Inf.* 3. 82 f.) retains this classical feature. There is, of course, no implication that Dante had knowledge of our piece: he did not have the Greek for that. Nevertheless, it is amusing to reflect that the Italian poet was coeval (1265–1321) with Constantine Acropolites, that stern denouncer of the *Timarion*'s very similar blending of pagan and Christian ingredients.

Inside the gate, more guards greet the devils and their charge. Hades is apparently run on efficient lines, for Timarion is both expected and recognized, and his reason for being there is also on file.

The pace now slackens to a leisurely stroll, and Timarion's package tour of hell gets underway. He finds himself in a mean-looking suburbia of poor and crowded tents or shacks. Thanks to the respect with which the devils are greeted by their inhabitants, our hero is in no danger of losing his way or getting mugged. People rise to their feet in awe of his guides, like boys in the presence of their teachers. Is this a subtle way of saying that Byzantine pedagogues were regarded as diabolical by their pupils? One thinks of the classics master in Rattigan's *Browning Version,* nicknamed the Himmler of the Lower Fifth.

At various intervals throughout the satire, Timarion meets and describes a particular individual. Usually these are not named, but verbal clues or other pointers to their identities are given that a contemporary reader could presumably grasp. The first such character now appears. He seems to have been connected to the family of the governor in Thessalonica. Living alone in Hades, he reclines in a well-lighted place, shovelling pork and cabbage into his mouth. Gluttony, a regular motif of classical satire, is one of the dominant themes of Byzantine humour, and the *Timarion* is no exception.

Gluttony is traditionally a solitary vice, but the old man is actually not quite alone. He amiably offers Timarion a share of the grub, but the latter is repelled by the sight of two fat mice waiting to jump in his beard and lick at the food droppings therein. A Saturday morning cartoon motif, if ever there was one.

At the next vision, thought for food gives way to food for thought. Timarion is drawn to a well-lit, shining white tent by the deep groaning from within. In it he finds a recumbent figure whose eyes have been gouged out and from whose mouth drops of poison trickle down. This pitiable creature is the late emperor Romanus IV Diogenes, who, having lost the great battle of Manzikert against the Turks in 1071, was dethroned on his return home and was blinded with especial barbarity.

We have a full account of all this from the contemporary historian Michael Psellus, who will crop up in the *Timarion* later as chief clerk of the court. Our narrator gets his information from a passing shade, who, perceiving from his residual colour that Timarion is newly arrived, trades this information for news about the latest food prices in the city. Quite why Romanus should be one of the only two emperors named in the satire is uncertain, though the fact that he hailed from Cappadocia would suit Timarion's own origins. As we have seen, the reference cannot be an exactly contemporary one. Just possibly, the defeat of Romanus was recognised then as a turning point in Byzantine history as it is now.

Going on his merry way, Timarion is next accosted by a tall, white-haired and shrivel-faced man who talks and laughs a lot. Having peered closely at him for some time, this character recognises and greets the narrator as his old and favourite pupil. In return, Timarion recognises his old master, the famous rhetorician and glutton, Theodore of Smyrna.

Readers of Dante will recognise the scene as very similar to that in the *Inferno* (15. 22 f.) where the poet meets Brunetto Latini. Theodore of Smyrna was a real person. He will remain with Timarion for the rest of the adventure. A volubly cheerful chap, he tells the narrator, who, having been his pupil, should have known anyway, that he was the top rhetorical performer at court but then ate himself to death. There is a touch of Rumpole of the Bailey in Pommeroy's wine bar about this, as there is in the consolation he finds in death: the meagre diet of cress, mallows, and asphodel have restored his health and figure.

Professor and pupil exchange their stories in detail, a palpably clumsy device on the author's part. Their relationship is maintained, Timarion pleading inexperience in law and asking Theodore to undertake his case. The latter is only too glad to agree, being anxious to have a go against the great medical men of the past, not to mention Aesculapius, who together are a permanent board of expert advisers to the infernal court.

This all reflects the doctrinal and professional squabbles between doctors, lawyers, philosophers, and rhetoricians in Byzantium. So does Timarion's anxiety lest he, a Christian, not get fair treatment from the pagan judges, Aeacus and Minos. Although paganism had long been dead as a force, it was still common for Byzantines to level the term as one of abuse against a theological rival.

Theodore assures him that all will be well. He looks forward to wrestling the doctors to the ground, especially as Galen, the most formidable of them all, is away in a corner of Hades revising his book on the differences between fevers, a possible allusion to some new edition of his works in Constantinople. As to the judges, not to worry; they now have a Christian colleague to set them right.

He comes as a surprise. It is the former emperor Theophilus, the last of the iconoclast emperors, whose death in 842 marked the end of that bitter, century-long controversy over icons. Theophilus had enjoyed a reputation for honesty and fair dealing, but it remains striking that this heretic should so long after his death be a byword for virtue in orthodox Byzantium, especially in light of the strictness of the Comnenan emperors of the time.

Equally eye-catching is the term Timarion uses for the Christians. He calls them "Galilaeans," an epithet always used by Julian, the apostate emperor, in his effort to demean the sect by stressing its geographical insignificance. This section, then, may be the most daring in satirical terms, and it is no surprise that Constantine Acropolites should have singled it out for his animadversions.

The two are now conducted by the devils to an oasis of light and greenery about two miles away, wherein the court is located. A paradise is there described in varyingly earthly terms. It sounds partly like classical Elysium, partly like California, save that spring rather than summer is the season of eternal delight. Albeit a traditional detail, this makes sense, given the climate in Istanbul. It also resembles Dante's Earthly Paradise.

Timarion's trial has to wait for the conclusion of the one they find in session. This is a real eyebrow-raiser: Brutus and Cassius impeached for their murder of Julius Caesar. Why have they only now come to court, more than a thousand years later? Romano sees in this a delicate allusion to the possibility that the emperor John Comnenus' death whilst hunting in 1143 was actually murder. If so, that gives us another clue to the date of the satire. The notion might be supported by the fact that Timarion does not hear what the verdict is. On the other hand, although Roman history does not much feature in Byzantine satire, it may only be a traditional *exemplum*. Dante, it will be remembered, puts Brutus and Cassius along with Judas Iscariot in the lowest reach of hell (*Inf.* 34. 61 f.).

That case over, it is the turn of Timarion versus the devils, whose names we now learn to be Oxybas and Nyktion. The trio of judges assemble, Theophilus standing out for his austere dress, a contrast to the glitter of his pagan colleagues, and his adviser, a sexless and simpering angel in white. One commentator (Tozer) finds this a slightly profane notion, but there is support for it in patristic writing.

Theodore pleads his pupil's case with force, demanding a forensic inspection of his client's soul which establishes that the body had not entirely lost all its element of bile and that therefore the devils had acted prematurely in bringing him down. Since the medical advisers are no help to the accused, and as Minos in Queen of Hearts style had started shouting at the devils even before their evidence was heard, the quality of infernal justice does not seem beyond improvement. This looks like satire upon a real-life theme.

After an adjournment, predictably spent eating by Theodore and Timarion, the judges return and find for the prosecution. Timarion may return to earth and live out his allotted span. He will be conducted there by the court ushers, who assume the devils' job, the hapless devils themselves being deposed from office.

This sentence is read by the clerk of court, the lisping Byzantine sophist, that is to say, Michael Psellus. He is brought in a little later as well to join in the discussions of philosphers and rhetoricians observed by Timarion on his journey back. A series of such vignettes, notably a verbal and physical slugfest between Diogenes the Cynic and the philosopher John Italus, finally broken up by the Roman Cato, allows the author to satirise in Lucianic style the intellectual sects of his day.

As they approach the exit from hell, Theodore of Smyrna takes leave of the narrator, but not before handing him a shopping list of foods to be sent down: a five-month-old lamb, two three-year-old fowls, a one-month-old sucking pig, and a fat sow's belly. It is clear that his subterranean diet is about to be broken with a vengeance.

Unlike Dante and the writers of many classical descents into hell, the author of the *Timarion* is not much concerned with grisly descriptions of the tortures of the damned. There is, however, one gesture in this direction. Just before leaving, our hero glimpses a trio of villains: Alexander of Pherae from Greek history; Philaretus, an Armenian usurper of the eleventh century; and Nero, the Anti-Christ (though that is not the author's own phrase). A textual problem makes it uncertain whether it is all three or just Nero who is undergoing the fate of shovelling excrement, a condign punishment meted out by Dante to the flatterers (*Inf.* 18. 107 f.).

The ushers conduct Timarion back up the pit. He sees the stars with relief but still needs help in finding his body, which by now of course is cold. He enters the lodging house through the chimney, which is described in so contorted a way as possibly to imply that this is a novel feature in Byzantine houses, and reenters his corpse via nostrils and mouth. After a chilly night, he is recovered enough on the morrow to pack his bags and return home. He instructs Kydion to give the foods promised to Theodore to a couple of newly departing dead, preferably filthy Paphlagonians from the market. After which, justifiably tired, and no doubt fearing another flood of questions from Kydion, he ends his tale with the time-honoured formula whereby parents get rid of their children: and so to bed.

BYZANTINE CRITICISM OF THE *TIMARION*

In *BZ* 1 (1982), 361–5, the German scholar M. Treu published a letter to an unnamed friend by the statesman Constantine Acropolites, the sole concern of which is to denounce the *Timarion* and its author for impiety. This letter (also in Romano 42–45) contains a number of ambiguous and obscure expressions but runs something along the following lines:

> Considering that the author of the *Timarion* was an oldish barbarian who came late in life to catch up with things here in Constantinople, I will not dwell on the deficiencies of his general education, but will go so far as to admit that he did manage to get a small taste, at least to the tip of his forefinger, of eloquence and culture, also that this superficial acquaintance with the art of rhetoric resulted in his achieving a quite respectable prose style whose Greek was grammatical and even possessed of a certain Attic panache. But as for the more spiritual elements of the true knowledge, the knowledge which adds that vital spark to the mere mastery of technique, well, to judge from the viewpoint of one who has acquired at least the rudiments, he remained quite devoid of those, and equally failed to achieve that skill and grace in dialogue which in my experience is one of the key ingredients in the work of true thinkers.
>
> Worse, although having this degree of technical expertise in the theory and practise of rhetoric, he came up with the miserable volume I have before me. Truly, as Homer

says, this Timarion deserves to be valued at but a single straw for producing such stuff. I cannot imagine what motivated him to attack the Christian faith. It is all the more strange since, by starting with the festival of the famous martyr St Demetrius, he did make a good and appropriately solemn start before degenerating into his quite unsuitable tale. Did I say unsuitable? Raving lunacy would be a better description. Why, this thunderstruck fool, this certifiable maniac, wanted to revive the myths of the pagans, though he was shrewd enough to assume the veneer of a Christian refuting open error and commending true belief and, if I may put it so, laying out the tenets of true orthodoxy before the eyes of those that can see, whilst all the time his intention was to string together pagan nonsense in an incompatible union with the truth and to make light of things that should properly induce awe since they proceed from the one true perception of God.

True, I felt pity for the man, if that is the right word for him, but more than pity I feel disgust at the nonsense he has produced under his veneer of learning and cloak of piety as his legacy for posterity. And as for his putting judges of pagan descent in authority over those whom the Lord and Creator redeemed with his own blood and on whom he conferred the supreme honour of his name and calling, what madness does this not surpass? With what known type of insanity can it possibly be compared? Why, this creature has gone beyond the bounds even of those notorious scoundrels Margites and Coroebus, for they innocently transgressed against the Passion, but he did it knowingly and willingly.

They, indeed, since they knew not what they did, might reasonably be thought to deserve some pity. But this fellow seems to me to be utterly abominable and should so seem to his contemporaries and posterity, since he did not fall into error but gladly embraced it. Wherefore, as soon as I had got to the end of his book, I felt I should consign it to the flames so that in the future it would not fall into the hands of any Christian. And my intention would have become a *fait accompli* had not the sense of respect for a fellow believer which I have long maintained intervened to

> stop me. This held my hand, so to speak, and restrained
> me from my intent, thus saving this insane book from the
> fate which I think it so richly deserves.
>
> So, my godlike friend, I have disclosed to you what I
> think about the enclosed volume. In return, I want very
> much to have your opinion.

Strong stuff. We do not know who this friend was, or what,
if anything, was his reply. Acropolites certainly numbered
some important men among his many correspondents. The
information about his life and writings is conveniently assembled by D. M. Nicol, *DOP* 19 (1965), 249–56. Briefly, Constantine Acropolites was the son of the statesman and historian
George Acropolites (1217–82). He was appointed logothete
around 1282 by Andronicus II and was promoted in 1294 or
thereabouts to the office of grand logothete (in effect, con-
troller of the entire civil service), a position he held until at
least 1321. He is known from a monastery record to have been
dead by 1324. Apart from his duties of state, he was active in
religious life, founding a monastery and taking an outspoken
position in his earlier years against the policy of union with the
Church of Rome then being pursued by Michael VIII. He was
a prolific hagiographer and epistolographer; cf. H. Delehaye,
AB 51 (1933), 263–84, for a selection of his letters, many of
which remain unpublished.

The letter in front of us has an obvious bearing on the question of the *Timarion*'s date and will feature in my discussion of
that issue in the next section. At stake here are his opinions on
the satire. The modern reader may well think Acropolites
madder than the object of his spleen. But as our earlier survey
showed, the Byzantines went in for this intemperate language
in a big way. He is not very specific on what he finds so
impious about the work, apart from the mingling of pagan and
Christian elements and the use of pagan judges in the underworld sequences. As my commentary will discuss, other details
that may have outraged him could include the use of "Galilaean" for Christian, the notion of religious freedom, and a
seemingly flippant allusion to the Resurrection.

No modern reader will consider the *Timarion* subversive. More to the point, it is tame by Byzantine standards in some respects, when compared to the brutal personal attacks on politicians in the *Mazaris,* the sharp comments on social problems in Alexius Macrembolites' *Dialogue between the Rich and the Poor* (written about twenty years after Acropolites' death), and the aforementioned *Office or Mass of a Beardless Man* with its profanities. However, Acropolites was not an isolated bigot. In his day, the old issue of how to reconcile Hellenism with Christian piety—an issue as venerable as Tertullian, Jerome, and Basil—was again a lively one. The reader is referred for details to D. M. Nicol, "The Byzantine Church and Hellenic Learning in the Fourteenth Century," *Church History* 5 (1969), 23–57, reprinted in his collected essays *Byzantium: Its Ecclesiastical History and Relations with the Western World* (London, 1972) and synthesised in his *Church and Society in the Last Centuries of Byzantium* (Cambridge, 1979), 31–65. In short, two themes raised by Acropolites are mythology and the mingling of pagan with Christian elements. These were issues much debated in late Byzantium. On one side was the ideal of fusing the two, propounded by (for instance) Theodore II Lascaris around 1250. On the other, Isidore, patriarch of Constantinople (1347–50; 1355–63) deemed Greek myths unsuitable for Christian students; so did "the holy fool" Sabas of Vatopedi, who singled out mythology as pure nonsense.

Viewed in this light, the diatribe of Acropolites was simply part of an everlasting debate over the fundamentals of Byzantine intellectual life. To us, the object of his attack seems singularly ill-chosen; on the broader issue, he was emphatically not a lunatic operating in isolation. Beyond this, his letter has its own interest as a specimen of literary criticism by one Byzantine of a *secular* piece of writing by another. The modern reader would also like to know how many other Byzantines shared Acropolites' view of the *Timarion*. Was it widely discussed in the fourteenth century? No other extant work mentions it. Does its survival in a single manuscript imply that it was subject to burning, a piece of samizdat literature? Not really; other ancient works, including noncontroversial ones, have survived by an equally slender thread. Finally, there is the question of the light the letter may or may not shed on the date of the *Timarion,* a matter for the next section.

THE DATE AND AUTHORSHIP OF THE *TIMARION*

Though by no means a unique situation, it is exasperating that neither the precise date nor the author of the *Timarion* are known. It will be seen that our ignorance of the latter is more profound; a general date can be argued on reasonably solid grounds. We are probably more frustrated by the authorship issue than a Byzantine would be. As Cyril Mango, *Byzantium: The Empire of New Rome,* 240–1, puts it, "The Byzantines showed little interest in their own literature and none whatever in the biography of their writers, which is why we know so little about them." Playing Guess the Author tends to be a futile scholarly parlour game. But the reader needs to know about the various dates and candidates that have been proposed, and why. Also, educated guesswork can provoke worthwhile debate and may on occasion provide the vital clue for someone else to follow up.

Disputes over date and authorship are unavoidably complex and hard for the Greekless to follow when, as here, linguistic data are part of the argument. I have kept this element to the minimum to avoid boredom and with the plan of publishing a more technical version elsewhere. To help keep the reader's mind clear as to who thinks what, without hopelessly cluttering up the text with parentheses, I have equipped this section with a few basic footnotes.

I am by no means the first to locate the *Timarion* in the twelfth century. This date is commonplace in handbooks and surveys of Byzantine literature,[1] and is the one acknowledged by its editors Hase, Ellissen, and Romano. Which part of the twelfth century, however, is quite another matter, with (for instance) Browning assigning it to the beginning, Vasiliev to the middle, and Cheetham[2] within the limits of the reign of Manuel I (1143–80). None of these scholars equip their precision with arguments. Equally lacking in explanation are the more radical dissentients, Kyriakis,[3] who puts the satire in the eleventh century, and Constantelos,[4] who ascribes it to the fourteenth. These conflicting claims demand a fresh and full look at the evidence.

So also does the authorship, where there is a similar situation. Most handbooks consider the work anonymous. But in recent years, at least three individual candidates have been proposed: Timarion, Theodore Prodromos, and Nicolas Callicles. Their claims, along with those of any other possibles, require the same sort of scrutiny.

First, the date. There are only two external clues. As earlier seen, the one manuscript containing the *Timarion* belongs to the fourteenth or early fifteenth century. More to the point, the letter of Constantine Acropolites must have been written by 1324, since we know he was dead by then. This does not leave much room in the fourteenth century to accommodate the chronology of Constantelos, although there is obviously enough. That scholar presumably understood Acropolites to be reacting to a recently published work. Other things being equal, this would have been a reasonable, even attractive, notion. Unfortunately, Acropolites' references to the object of his attack are from any point of view ambiguous. He gives the impression of having only just come across a work known to very few others. But this does not prove contemporaneity: Byzantine secular literature enjoyed limited audiences and was quick to go out of date. Moreover, Byzantine critics use very similar language in their attacks on such long-dead writers as Lucian. Again, when Acropolites says that the author deserves the hatred of both his own time and posterity, that could (as expressed in the Greek) refer either to the past and the present, or to the present and the future. By the same token, Acropolites' seeming lack of any knowledge of the author himself need not mean that the satire came from the past: anonymity would explain his ignorance. But against this, we have seen that Byzantine critics had little interest in the biography of authors, and therefore we cannot assume that Acropolites' silence is the product of ignorance; it could just as easily be indifference. The most compelling argument against Constantelos' date is the simple fact that all the discernible characters and incidents in the *Timarion* clearly belong to the late eleventh and twelfth centuries.

Of these, we may first consider a quintet of historical personages who appear in the satirist's Hades as dead men. These characters, all fully discussed in my commentary, are:

1. Romanus IV Diogenes, who died in 1072.
2. Philaretus, an Armenian general datable to the period 1072–86.
3. Michael Psellus, the year of whose death is not known but which is generally put around 1078, the time at which his *Chronography* breaks off.
4. John Italus, who fades from our sight after his trial in 1082 but on the evidence of Anna Comnena 5. 9 lived on for an unspecified time afterwards.
5. Theodore of Smyrna, who was certainly alive in 1112, a fact that rules out the eleventh century date of Kyriakis. When Theodore of Smyrna died is not known, but there is a possible pointer, so far overlooked. In the two summaries of his career given in the *Timarion* (chs. 24, 39), he is said to have lectured to and received great honour and patronage from Their Majesties. In both cases, the Greek has the plural of *basileus*. The question is, do we take this to mean "emperors" or "emperor and empress?" Romano, who offers no comment, translates *degli imperatori* on both occasions. Certainly, this plural can indicate emperor and wife; it is so used by Anna Comnena 3. 3 (actually in the archaic grammatical "dual" form indicating a natural pair) of Alexius I and Eirene. On the other hand, the early Byzantine historian Procopius distinguished between *basileus* and *basilissa* even in such a passage as *Buildings* 1. 9. 5, where he emphasises that Justinian and Theodora shared power and did everything in common.

As a ruler who, in the words of Anna Comnena 6. 7, tried to rekindle the flame of learning, Alexius will have been obliged to pay attention to the occupant of the sophist's chair, even though his own chief interest was the reading and exegesis of Scripture (Anna 14. 7). As to Eirene, Anna (5. 9) tells us that she always read the Scriptures along with the works of Maximus Confessor, "for she was not so much interested in scientific enquiry (*physikas syzeteseis*) as theology (*dogmata*)." Now scientific treatises of this sort were precisely the sort of study Theodore himself engaged in.[5] One might then surmise that Eirene would not have been a willing listener to discourses on such themes. But this would not be conclusive. *Noblesse oblige* might have compelled her attendance, and Theodore's intervention in the theological dispute with the Latins should have earned (indeed, might have been designed to earn) her favour.

The point is, if the plural refers to more than one emperor, they would have to be Alexius and his successor John II Comnenus (1118–43), since thanks to the tenures of Psellus and John Italus, Theodore cannot be fitted into any preceding reign as consul of the philosophers. On this reckoning, he was active after 1118, which would push the *Timarion* further down the twelfth century.

With regard to John II Comnenus, another clue has been divined. When Timarion gets to the judgement seat (ch. 31), he has to wait for the conclusion of the trial in session, that of Brutus and Cassius for the murder of Julius Caesar. Romano wonders if this flagrant anachronism might not be a covert allusion to John's sudden death by foul play in 1143.[6] This would obviously move the *Timarion* down at least to the reign of Manuel I, presumably early in his reign while John's death was still a talking point in Constantinople. The idea might be supported by Timarion's failure to give the result of the trial, possibly the silence of a prudent man. But there are objections. As Romano himself admits, Brutus and Cassius are something of a moral exemplar. Also, the scene in the *Timarion* has a literary pedigree based on Lucian, the author's favourite model; cf. my note 183 for details on all of this.

The quick as well as the dead are also relevant. Early in the satire (chs. 7–9), the author obtrudes a detailed, indeed wearisome, eulogy of the governor at Thessalonica. This individual used confidently to be identified with Michael Palaeologus Ducas, a general restored to favour by Manuel I after exile at the hands of John II, who is known to have died on campaign in Italy in 1156. Such an equation would probably locate the *Timarion* between the accession of Manuel and 1156. However, more recent scholarship (cf. my note 63 for full details) has shown that this identification is not certain.

References to people, then, provide no decisive clue to the date, though they do eliminate the eleventh century from contention and overall provide a panorama that fits the twelfth but no later. A couple of less tangible items may be canvassed, if only to stimulate further discussion. First, it might be a reasonable presumption that the author's description of Thessalonica predates the brutal sack of that city in 1185. But such a notion is weakened by the unfortunate tendency of Byzantine literature to ignore contemporary events; cf. my note 23 for a full discussion.

Secondly, Timarion is rebuked (ch. 3) by his interlocutor Kydion for going too fast in his narrative, "as though you are being pursued by dogs or Scythians." The latter is a typical Byzantine archaism, an irritating trick of style that goes back to the historians of the fourth and fifth centuries A.D. Here it is natural to take the term as denoting the Petchenegs (or Patzinaks) of South Russia. They were defeated by the Byzantines in 1091, and again in 1122; cf, my note 20. If we could be sure that Scythian stood for Petcheneg, their mention might furnish a clue to the date of the *Timarion,* since they cease to be a threat after 1122.[7] But since the author later (ch. 22) dubs the Seljuk Turks "Eastern Scythians," the identification cannot be certain.

There is not more that can fruitfully be said about the date. The reader is now in a position to appreciate the nature and limitations of the evidence. I will simply restate my own belief in a twelfth century date, and move on to the question of authorship. Even if we cannot be more precise, the twelfth century date has the advantage of restricting the field of candidates. Three have been so far proposed.

1. Timarion himself. That is, the narrator is equated with the author. This simple (to say simplistic would be unfair) solution is that of Dräseke and has the powerful support of Vasiliev.[8] It might gain strength from the fact that Acropolites simply refers to the dialogue by its narrator and seems not to know any other authorial name. This, of course, need only mean that the piece was, or had become, anonymous. If correct, the notion would on internal evidence equip the author with Cappadocian origins and a sophistic career in Constantinople. The fact that he would be otherwise unknown is no obstacle to acceptance; such a situation is not uncommon with ancient authors.

2. Theodore Prodromos. There are many references to this versatile man of letters in my notes; see especially 234. H. Hunger suggested Prodromos as the author in his edition of the latter's satire *Battle of the Mice*.[9] The grounds are partly syllogistic—Prodromos wrote satires in the Lucianic vein—and partly linguistic, a long list of words and phrases common to Prodromos and the *Timarion* being produced in support. Interestingly in this latter connection, Romano, who uses the same sort of argument in favour of his candidate, observed no parallels in his commentary. The appeal to linguistic similarities is a common scholarly device, but it is one that has very obvious frailties. Especially when, as here, the words in question are such simple ones (e.g. *arti*, "just now"; *ai ai,* "oh dear"; *kakistos,* "the worst"; and so on). In brief, there are two factors which seriously weaken both Hunger's and Romano's statistics: a) the words and phrases are often to be found in other Byzantine writers of the period; b) almost all the words in both their lists were used by Lucian, the common model of Prodromos and the *Timarion*. My commentary provides details of many such coincidences. In addition, Prodromos is addicted to neologisms and rare words, the author of the *Timarion* is not; cf. my note 33 for details and discussion. Finally, Hunger's equa-

tion is naturally incompatible with the usual view that Prodromos himself is ridiculed in the *Timarion*, ch. 43, though I myself do not think he is; cf. my note 234 for the arguments.

3. Nicolas Callicles. This doctor and poet of the time of Alexius I (he was at that emperor's deathbed) is the choice of Romano.[10] His candidate bids fair to become the orthodoxy in that it has attracted the favour (insofar as they mention it without overt criticism) of several distinguished scholars.[11] Romano's arguments seem to me to be surprisingly weak, being as follows:

a) The author celebrates the governor of Thessalonica, a member of the Palaeologus and Ducas families, and Callicles deplores the death of one male member thereof in poems 6–10. But almost anyone in twelfth-century Byzantium, especially literary hacks or men looking for patrons, would want to be on the right side of so powerful a group. And in fact, it is easy to find such praises in the literature of the age.[12]

b) Callicles mentions an unnamed "man from Smyrna," as does Theophylact of Bulgaria (*Ep.* 57. ed. Meurs = *PG* 126. 476C) in a letter to Callicles himself. This may indeed be Theodore of Smyrna, as Romano[13] thinks. But the consul of the philosophers, as Theodore was after 1082, enjoyed a regular circle of literary disciples and friends, all of whom would know each other. Theodore Prodromos, for easy and pertinent example, salutes Callicles at the end of his satire *Executioner or Doctor;* so does the author of the Third Beggar Poem.[14]

c) The author of the *Timarion* "ha buone conoscenze di medicina," which makes Callicles a likely candidate since he was teacher of the doctors (*didaskalos ton iatron*) and one of the physicians attending the fatal illness of Alexius I. For a refutation of the basis of this argument, see my note 87.

d) Callicles has a good knowledge of Roman history, citing Scipio, Catulus, and Scaurus; the *Timarion* mentions Brutus and Cassius, Cato, and Nero. But this proves nothing. Both authors are drawing on their stock of *exempla*. Scipio was a particularly easy one, being available for the taking in Lucian, *Dialogues of the Dead* 12; cf. *The Long-Lived* 12 (whether or not by Lucian is debated). Scipio is the only Roman invoked by the seventh-century poet George of Pisidia.[15] The letters and other prose writings of Theodore Prodromos are liberally sprinkled with names from Roman history (e.g. *Epp.* 1, 5, 8). Contemporary historians, for instance Anna Comnena (1. 1) and Nicephorus Bryennius (2. 3), also very naturally import such Roman references. They cannot be called a distinguishing feature of any one individual's style.

Romano's other arguments depend upon linguistic parallels, and have been criticised above in connection with Hunger's similar ones for Theodore Prodromos.

It may finally be pointed out that Romano's theory requires a presumption that the medical man Nicolas Callicles was capable of satirising his own profession. He would also have to be able to make fun of his own views, since Anna Comnena 15. 11 mentions his adherence to the humoral theory; cf. my note 87. This is naturally not impossible, but it is a factor to be weighed, especially as there is no hint of such a personality in the account of Callicles given by Anna. Not that the deathbed of an emperor was the place for levity, but it is unlikely that the serious Anna would have written so approvingly of a man known for irreverent wit.[16]

Such are the pros and cons of the various theories. Having been negative towards the ideas of fellow scholars, it is my duty as well as my pleasure to end on a positive note. There are two further possibilities that might be canvassed. First, bearing in mind Lucian's habit of calling himself Lycinus rather than Lucianus,[17] it is conceivable that the author of the *Timarion*, for whom Lucian was of course the prime model, did likewise. On that reckoning, we should look for a name not Timarion but a recognisable allotrope.

Secondly, it should be kept in mind that the twelfth century was rich in satiric spirits. Theodore Prodromos is only the best known. John Tzetzes would have been capable of the *Timar-*

ion, but I doubt that vain man could have hidden his light under the bushel of anonymity. And linguistically, as with Prodromos, the *Timarion* is too sparing of neologism and rarity to suggest his authorship. Nicephorus Basilaces[18] is known to have written four verse satires and a speech, *Against Bagoas,* whose title suggests a comic attack. As a rhetorician turned theologian and then deposed by the patriarch from the post of *didaskalos tou apostolou* in 1156, he had the right sort of career and misfortunes. So did Basileios Pediates, dismissed from a teaching position and a diaconate in 1168 for writing "blasphemous verses full of impiety."

The most attractive candidate, however, might be Michael Italicus.[19] His dates are right: he belongs to the reigns of John II and Manuel I. More objectively, he suits many of Romano's own criteria, thus: a) he was patronised by Eirene Ducas, widow of Alexius I, to whom he wrote a letter still extant; b) he was also in a position to pen addresses to the emperors John and Manuel, and possibly (these works are of uncertain attribution) monodies on the sons of Alexius I and John; c) he had the right sort of medical knowledge, being *didaskalos ton iatron* and author of a monody on Michael Pantechnes, court physician along with Nicolas Callicles and others to Alexius I. He also held a post as teacher of rhetoric, and was a literary polymath; d) his letters are sprinkled with allusions to Roman history: Antony and Cleopatra (*Ep.* 7), Marcus Aurelius (*Ep.* 17), the emperor Tiberius (*Ep.* 22), Scipio Africanus and Pompey in a sketch of Roman history (*Ep.* 28); e) there are one or two linguistic parallels between him and the *Timarion:* in addition to those discussed in my notes 186 and 188, notice the nonpejorative use of *polypragmoneo* (*Ep.* 2; cf. my note 60), the idiom *eipen an* (*Epps.* 6, 21; cf. Romano 29), and the flood of rhetorical terms in *Ep.* 29, very similar to that in *Timarion* 44. Also, his letter to Theodore Prodromos is larded with the technical terms of rhetoric as well as allusions to pre-Socratic philosophers and to uncouth contemporary heretics, all features of the *Timarion.*

In addition, we might add that: a) whilst a Cappadocian connection cannot be established, Michael's tenure of the archbishopric of Philippolis would have given him the knowledge of travel in the provinces and the topography of Thrace manifest in the *Timarion;* b) the letter to him from Theodore Prodromos commends his description of the local mountains and rivers, something for which the *Timarion* goes in for in a big way, especially the latter; c) whilst it would be simplistic to infer a satiric spirit merely from his acquaintance with Prodromos, who was many other things as well, the connection is notable; d) so is the comic disquisition over the rival merits of cheese and bacon contained in another letter to Prodromos from Philippolis,[20] as well as his monody on a dead partridge.[21] In general terms, cf. *Ep.* 7, where satire is one of the many genres with which Michael toys; e) Michael Italicus had the requisite personality. He treated his medical appointment with some levity. He was once un-Byzantine enough (*Ep.* 25) to disparage a theological treatise for being unoriginal. In Browning's words, "He was a man of independent character and is often jocularly sceptical of much in Byzantine culture"; also,[22] "In his ability to stand outside of and criticise the cultural tradition which he so richly inherits, he was unusual in the 12th century."

I am not obsessed with the idea that Michael Italicus must be the author, and have no theories on other matters that require the equation. He is fanciable, and it is worth demonstrating that on Romano's own criteria Nicolas Callicles is not the only candidate that fits. If it encourages the reader to think for himself and provokes further debate, the time spent on the authorship question will not have been wasted.

TIMARION

KYDION. Well, if it isn't the great[1] Timarion.[2] So, "You
are here, Telemachus, sweet light of my life," as the poet[3]
says. But what on earth kept you away for so long? After all,
you did promise to come back quickly. In the words of the
poet[4] again, "Tell me all, don't be coy, put us both in the
picture." For you will be talking to a friend both old and new.[5]

TIMARION. My dear Kydion, you may have put me in
mind of the poems of Homer in your eagerness to find out
what has happened to me, but I shall also need the resources
of Greek Tragedy to tell my tale, to make my narrative even
more exquisite than my sufferings.[6]

KYDION. Oh, do get on with it and don't waste time, my
dear, dear Timarion. I am burning to know what happened to
you as it is, without you torturing me even more with all this
procrastinating.

TIMARION. "Alas, alas, why do you agitate and harass me
so?"[7] "Why take me from Troy," as the proverb goes? Better
yet, let me begin with a quote from Euripides'[8] description of a
similar situation: "There is nothing so terrible to tell, no suffering, no heaven-sent calamity, the weight of which humanity
may not have to bear." Or as the bard[9] puts it, "Earth bears
nothing that suffers more than mankind." My friend, if I were
to tell you the whole story, you would wish you had never
asked and that I had not told you what you wanted to know.

KYDION. Do get on[10] with your story, my good friend,
whilst there is still some sun shining brightly on you. It is
already time to feed the cows, and it would be a very good
idea for us to get home safely in the light of day, in case there
is something serious waiting for us.[11]

TIMARION. Well, my dear Kydion, I told you before how
pious and holy the object of my trip was, when I was saying
good-bye to you; so I shall not tell you any more about what
you already know. After we had said good-bye to you and had
set out from the city (i.e., Constantinople), some divine
providence[12] helped us along, smoothing our path and taking

care of every detail. To cut a long story short, it guaranteed that we were greeted and treated like sheiks, even though we looked more like philosophers in our drab clothes.[13] Nor did this providence overlook any of my friends or father's friends along the way. There was always someone to escort us both into and out the countryside.[14] We always found a slave, either one who met us by chance travelling along the same way, or one who happened to be busy ploughing along the roadside, to announce us to his master. In a word, everyone who saw us treated us hospitably.[15] Not that I need to spell out all the details of those lavish and delicious meals; I've already told you, they were positively oriental.[16] Indeed, my good friend, you will appreciate from the simple facts of the matter what sort of universal providence it is that provides the pleasures of life appropriate to those who have chosen the philosopher's *métier.* For though we hadn't stopped to think how we should eat after leaving home and had packed no food or drink,[17] we lacked for no comfort from the very first taste of hospitality. That's how it went on the outward journey, everything safe and sound. But it was a painfully different matter coming back, an absolute gothic horror story.[18]

3   KYDION. My friend, you have the most exasperating[19] way of telling a story, all précis and résumé, never really telling us what we want to know. For although you have not yet finished the account of your trip out, and have not told us a single thing about your stay, you are already rushing on to describe your return home. Anyone would think you were being chased by dogs or Scythians,[20] the way you are heading hell-for-leather in your tale to Constantinople itself, as though that were the only place in which you could find safety and escape from your pursuers. Come on, man. No dreadful fate is lying in wait for you, nothing bad will happen if you relax and give us the full story.

TIMARION. Damn your blessed insatiability, Kydion. What an incorrigible mania for travelogues you have. All right, I'll tell you what happened, as it happened, but do forgive me if I don't include such choice details as the crow that flew down at me, or the stone that dashed against the horses' hooves, or the bramble bush by the roadside that entangled us.

Well, we went down[21] to the world-famous[22] city of Thessalonica[23] before the beginning of the festival of St Demetrius the Martyr.[24] We were in high spirits[25] and fine fettle. We had some time to spare, thanks to not having to slave over our studies, and since idleness is to us what eating pork is to the Jews,[26] we went to the Axios River to hunt.[27]

This is the biggest river in Macedonia.[28] Originating in the Bulgarian mountains, it flows first in small and separate streams, then, contracting into a single basin for its descent, "bravely and well" as Homer[29] would say, it runs down towards old Macedonia and Pella[30] and empties itself immediately at the nearest shore. This area deserves quite a detailed description.[31] It has rich soil in which farmers can grow all sorts of crops. It is a good spot for cavalrymen to ride in, and an even better one for generals to practise battle manoeuvres in, being ideal for troop deployments since the phalanx is not broken up at all, thanks to the area being so entirely flat and free of stones and bushes. As to hunting, you could say that it is a place where Euripides' Phaedra, even if not madly in love with Hippolytus, might ride at her leisure and call to the hunting dogs and dart close to dappled deers.[32]

That's what the district around the Axios is like. And so I pleasantly whiled away the time before the festival hunting with my own friends and my father's. When the festival began, we went back[33] to the city. After we had visited the most sacred and holy places, where we paid the appropriate respects, we spent some time at the fair that was set up outside the city gates. It begins six days before the festival and ends promptly on the following Monday.[34]

4

KYDION. Our friend Timarion strikes again. He's back to his old form, even without realising it. His stories tend to have a beginning and an end but no middle.[35] And that's exactly what is happening right now. Just as though he's forgotten my request and his own promise, he looks as though he is going to bring his story to an end already by merely jumping from A to Z without giving us any details about the fair itself, its size and its splendour, or about all the people and the riches and all the things there were for sale. But, in the words of the bard,[36] "You don't get away from me, Menelaus, son of Atreus, whom the war god loves."

TIMARION. My dear Kydion, I'm afraid we shall have to spend the whole night here if I tell you everything you want to know. But what can I do? Friends' requests of this sort are tantamount to royal commands. One[37] can't get out of it, whatever it may be. So here goes, right back to the beginning.

5   The Demetria are a festival, just as the Panathenaia were in Athens and the Panionia amongst the Milesians.[38] And the fair is the most important held in Macedonia. Not only does the native and indigenous throng pour in but also men of every conceivable race and country. Greeks from wherever they happen to live, the entire motley crew of Mysians[39] who are our neighbours as far as the Danube and Scythia, Campanians, Italians in general, Iberians, Lusitanians, and Transalpine Celts.[40] In short, the shores of the ocean send pilgrims and sightseers to the martyr, so famous is he in Europe.

I myself, being just a Cappadocian[41] tourist from abroad, never having been to the fair before but only having heard about it, wanted to see everything there was to see at the same time, to make sure I didn't miss a thing. So I climbed up a hill[42] overlooking the fair where I could sit down and observe everything at leisure. And this is what there was. There were merchants' booths facing each other, set up in parallel rows. These rows extended for a long way and were far enough apart to form a walkway in the middle that was wide enough to allow space to move for the teeming crowd. Looking at the closeness of the booths and the evenness of their positioning, you could compare them to lines drawn over a long distance from two opposite points. At various points at an angle to the rows, other booths were set up. They were in rows as well, not long ones, but like the tiny feet that grow alongside reptiles' coils.[43] Indeed, although there were in fact two rows, the closeness and regularity of the booths created a quite remarkable illusion of a single living thing. One had the impression of a coil of booths, with the crossrows at the sides looking like the feet that supported it. In fact, as I love you,[44] when I contemplated the ground plan of all the booths from my vantage point, I couldn't help but compare it to a centipede with a very long body showing innumerable little feet under its belly.[45]

And, my curious Kydion, if you must know what I saw   6
inside after I had come down from the hill, there were all kinds of men's and women's clothes both woven and spun,[46] everything that comes from Boeotia and the Peloponnese, and all the things that merchant ships bring from Italy and Greece. Phoenicia also supplies many goods, as do Egypt, Spain, and the Pillars of Hercules, where the finest altar cloths are made. These items the merchants export directly from their respective countries to old Macedonia and Thessalonica. The Black Sea also contributes to the fair by sending across its own products to Constantinople, from where they are conveyed by large numbers of horses and mules.

I had a good close look through all these things after coming down. But whilst I was still sitting up on the hill, I was astonished at the number and types of the animals, and at their loud and confused noise which violently assaulted my ears. Whinnying horses, lowing cattle, bleating sheep, grunting pigs, and barking dogs following their masters as a defence against wolves and thieves.[47]

When I had had a good long look at all of this, long enough to satisfy my curiosity, I went back to the city very keen to see other things, above all the sacred gathering. This service is celebrated over three all-night vigils, with many priests and monks divided into two choirs constantly chanting the hymn in honour of the saint. The archbishop presides over these men as though he were the leader of an old-fashioned[48] embassy, supervising the festival and making sure that what should be done is done. These rites are performed throughout the night with the aid of torchlight.

"But when the early rising, rosy-fingered Dawn appears," to quote Homer,[49] the governor[50] of the land arrived at the church, advancing with a great and brilliant bodyguard, leading a procession of many cavalry and not a few infantry.[51]

7   As (in the words of Thucydides[52]) the populace stood agog in front of the entrance, eagerly awaiting his imminent presence, I went along with some rubberneckers from the crowd and met the procession at about one stade's (i.e. one-eighth of a mile) distance. It was a spectacle that gave me no ordinary delight. As to the motley crowd that was following it, both from the countryside and the city, I won't do more than mention its size. The chosen leaders, however—some might call them a veritable flotilla of clients—made the procession a marvellous sight, being men all in their prime, all glowing with health, all in fact the pupils and initiates of Enyalian Ares the war god, resplendent in their silk and studded garments, their hair thick and gold.[53] In fact, if you concentrated on their hair, you would be inclined to quote Homer[54] and say, "Their nature came from their heads" and "He let fall his thick locks that were like the hyacinth flower."

Beneath[55] them their Arabian horses pranced along, pawing the air and rearing up as though to leave the ground and fly.[56] They appeared to blend in with the surrounding splendour with all the gold and silver gleaming on their reins; as they kept arching their necks as though to display their glittering harnesses, it seemed as if they were enjoying[57] the gorgeousness of their trappings. That's how they looked as they advanced, making their way forward in orderly tempo and at military pace. After them there was a small interval before the governor rode up in an unhurried[58] style. Cupids, Muses, and Graces were scampering before him and under him.[59] Ah, my dear, dear Kydion, how could I ever describe to you the joy that entered my soul and the depth of my exaltation as I gazed upon him?

KYDION.   Well, my dear Timarion, do try at least to tell me who this man was, who his parents were, and how he appeared to your gaze as he came down the road. Tell me this, and everything else, in detail, remembering my original request that you do just that.

TIMARION.   His pedigree, as I found out by asking[60] those who knew, is heroic and fortunate on both parents' sides. His paternal grandfather was greatest of the great[61] in Great Phrygia, a man proudly wealthy and exalted in glory.[62] Indeed, the stories of old that were retailed either by himself or about him added a very old[63] title to his regular names. His father[64] was not only a man who knew many an ancient thing, as Homer[65] says, but one whose nobility came from his own achievements and whose great fame from his generalship. It was this very quality of leadership that brought him as his reward his beautiful wife, a lady who is in her own right greatest of the great, being of royal blood and descended from the famous Doukai family, a family whose fame, as you know, has been spread by the lips of many[66] across the sea from Italy and the race of Aeneas[67] to Constantinople itself. What man does not know of her father[68] of all men, distinguished as he is by his high offices of state, tested in the most important military commands, conferring[69] in every way an incomparable nobility upon his daughter? This is what I learned from the bystanders who knew his personal history, though it may well be that there was only time for them to tell me a few details out of many, a small part of a great story.[70] But let's pick up the thread of my story and get back to the procession.

So, as I was saying before, the flotilla of chosen men led the way. But then the continuity of the procession was broken like the snapping of a rope, and the great man was upon us in his full glory. In the words of Aristotle,[71] neither West nor East is so astonishing as was his epiphany. His[72] eyes sparkled like wine, his teeth were as white as milk. He was well-knit in body, tall, so beautifully proportioned in all his limbs that he lived up to what everyone said about him, namely, that there was no detail you would want to add or take away. His body, which was as tall and straight as a cypress tree, bent both upwards and downwards at the neck, as though Nature herself was keeping the curvature from irregularity and was keeping him nimble in every part. This, at any rate, was my first impression of him from a distance.

But when he had drawn close to us, and when we had made the formal recognition of his presence[73] that protocol demands, he resembled a veritable chameleon, completely incomparable. For like a potion that Homer[74] describes as containing many good ingredients and many bad, his appearance became variegated, at one moment projecting the grace of Aphrodite,[75] then, if you looked closely,[76] the vigour of Ares darted from his eyes, whilst a moment after that he gave off the great majesty of Zeus. In his eyes he resembled Hermes with his sharp and quick-changing glances, always keeping his gaze high up and ready to take in anything that came his way. He spoke in a style that was designed to be lucid[77] and persuasive. This was the full and true quality of his character as I saw it at close range. His hair was neither completely dark nor completely fair. The extremes of these two colours had been held in check, with the result that an entirely different hue gave his hair a marvellous tinge. For jet black is rough and unlovable, whilst pure blonde is womanly and effeminate, whereas the two together produce manliness and lovability.[78] A Sappho[79] must have contrived his speech to be full of its persuasion, grace, and musical cadence. You would have been dumbfounded, and would have come out with this classic Laconic[80] line, "Ye Gods,[81] a godlike man." And you would have given anything to hear him speak.

10   As this noble figure arrived at the holy sanctuary and offered the invocation to the martyr, cheering arose from the crowd as it made its customary act of devotion to the governor. Then he stood at the prescribed spot and bade the archbishop appear, a ritual that I suppose is also prescribed or customary.[82]

Then from those who had specially practiced[83] the rituals of the festival—what a congregation they had there—there was heard a most divine psalmody, most gracefully varied in its rhythm, order, and artistic alternations. For it was not only men who were singing; the holy nuns in the left wing[84] of the church, divided into two antiphonal choirs, also offered up the Holy of Holies to the martyr.[85] And when every part of the spectacle and service had been properly concluded, we too invoked the saint in the customary way, praying to the martyr for a safe return, after which we came out of the church along with the populace and the governor.

We went back to our lodgings. Ah, Kydion, what a gift of tongues I would need to describe to you the dreadful things that befell me after that. Look, I am quite beside myself in the mere telling of them, so how great do you imagine was the pain that actually afflicted me, transfixed as I was by such painful and baneful[86] diseases?

KYDION.   Just stick to our agreement, my dear Timarion, and tell me everything that happened to you, since you have at last managed to give me a decent account of everything else.

TIMARION.   Very well. After we had returned from the   11
festival to our usual lodgings, a violent fever[87] hit me. It lasted all night, leaving me half-dead and bedridden, eager though I was to begin my journey home. This, my dear Kydion, was the reason for my slowness that you questioned me about at the start of my story. For the best policy was to wait for the illness to run its normal course, along with applying the medications appropriate to each symptom.[88] Well, I got through that day all right by sticking to a diet of vegetables and vinegar.[89] But the next day, the third after it began, the fever hit me again, and by diagnosing it according to the strict principles of medical knowledge, I recognised it to be a genuine case of the tertian fever. So, making light of the sickness of which I expected to be quite cured by the time it got through its fifth cycle, which is the normal duration of this type of fever, I set out confidently for Constantinople, expecting to shake it off in a short while and arrive home safely.[90] Some hopes. The end of that fever turned out to be the beginning of my real agonies and the start of my death-like condition. For no sooner had

the fever let up when I was attacked by an inflammation of the liver and the most appalling dysentery, causing me to vomit up my elemental bile along with pure blood, as well as ravaging my flesh and biting into my stomach like a viper.[91]

12   It[92] was a case of many terrible woes combining against a single body. Travel fatigue in itself is no less capable than any disease of exhausting even the most robust constitution. The inflammation of the liver was like a furnace, the diarrhea was as bad as death itself. The acidity deep inside my gut was like iron nails digging in. On top of all that, there was my long period without food,[93] a sure route to death. So, my dear Kydion, transfixed as I was by all these woes, one of the pack horses carried me towards Constantinople strapped across its back like a parcel. For a long way, in fact for the greater part of the journey, my poor, wretched drained-out body managed to hold on. But when we got to the river Hebrus, which is the most famous river in Thrace, then I rested, not only from the journey, but from life itself. For I had come to the end of life's journey. Sleep, the father of death as they say, laid hold on me and took me down to Hades[94]—exactly how, I don't know. But I do know this, fear and trembling are coming over me as I recollect what happened, and my vocal cords are seizing up out of fear.

KYDION. They may be seizing up, Timarion, but you won't manage to dissolve this assembly of ours without telling me what precisely did happen to you on this trip to Hades.

13   TIMARION. Very well, my dear Kydion. Since my poor body was completely worn out by the dysentery, and even more so by going twenty[95] full days without food, I began, so it seemed, to sleep the last sleep. Now, there are in the universe certain avenging spirits, as they have been called, who are appointed by divine providence to punish those who transgress against the laws of God. There are also benevolent spirits who reward the good. In addition to these, there are conductors of souls[96] whose mission it is to bring down by whatever way they can the souls that have already[97] left their bodies to Pluto,

Aeacus, and Minos[98] so that they may undergo examination according to the customs and laws of the dead before being allotted their destiny and destination.

This is precisely what happened to me. Just before midnight, some shadowy, dusty-looking creatures came flying through the air and landed on my bed where I was stretched out trying to sleep.[99] As soon as I saw them, I froze at the weirdness of the sight. I did my best to scream, but my voice was paralysed and my powers of speech wouldn't work. Was it a dream, or did it really happen? That I cannot say, since terror had also robbed me of my faculty of judgement. Whatever it was, it was so clear, so awfully clear. Indeed, it seems even now to be right in front of my eyes, so frightful was it what happened to me then.[100] For having placed, as it were, an unbreakable gag over my tongue, either by the awfulness of the sight or by some mysterious spell, they stood over me and began to whisper to each other, saying, "This is the man who lost the fourth of his constituent elements by vomiting up all his bile. He cannot be allowed to go on living on the strength of the remaining three. Aesculapius[101] and Hippocrates have said as much in the decree they wrote down and posted up in Hades whereby no man, even if his body be in good shape, shall go on living if he has been deprived of one of his four elements." "So," they went on in harsher tones, "follow us, you poor devil, and join the ranks of your fellow dead,[102] since that is what you now are yourself."

I had to follow them. I didn't want to, of course, but having no help I had no choice. I was transported through the air the same as they were; I became light, nimble, weightless, my legs unimpeded[103] so that I went forward lightly and without any problems, like ships that run before the wind.[104] You could hear a light rushing sound as I zoomed along, similar to the whizzing noise that arrows make when they are shot from bows. When we had crossed that river we hear about, without getting wet, and also the Acherusian Lake[105]—a name, incidentally, which my guides also used—we approached a subterranean opening, much larger than the one wells have. The

14

darkness that was visible from the mouth was foul and horrible.[106] I didn't want to go down there, but my guides separated and sandwiched me between them until one of them went headfirst down the opening and dragged me after him with a fierce look. I resisted as best I could, clinging to the mouth with hands and feet until the other guide who was following behind hit me across the cheeks with his knuckles and beat me over the back as well, thus forcing me with both his hands down that dark pit.

Once inside, we journeyed a long way in darkness and solitude[107] until we came at last to the iron gate[108] by which the realm of Hades is closed off. It is quite impossible for anyone who has once entered to escape from it. That gate is a truly terrifying thing in its size and weight and massive wrought iron. The whole thing is made out of unbreakable iron, with no wood at all, and it is reinforced throughout by iron bars that are themselves unbelievable in their size and weight and thickness of circumference.

15   On guard outside it were dragons[109] with fiery eyes and a dog with very sharp teeth whom the Greeks of old used to call Cerberus,[110] a very fierce and terrifying animal. Inside it were the doorkeepers, gloomy and unsmiling men, darting forth looks of pure hatred, looking rough and weather-beaten as though they had just come down from a life of banditry in the mountains. But for all their fierce expressions, they opened the gates with alacrity on seeing the conductors of the dead. Cerberus, wagging his tail this way and that, fawned and rubbed himself against them, whilst the dragons hissed gently as my guides led me forward quite unresisting. For, as I said before,[111] having no help I had no choice, especially now that I had been brought into such a strange and terrifying world. When I had been brought forward, the doorkeepers looked keenly at me and said, "This is the man Aeacus and Minos were talking about yesterday, the very man who had lost his fourth element and who was trying to keep on living on the strength of the other three, without his bile, in defiance of the prescription of Hippocrates and Aesculapius and the rest of

the medical profession. Bring in this wretch, whatever his own theories about the composition of the body may be. For how can it be all right for a man to carry on living in the upper world along with normal men if he hasn't got all four elementary humours?"

KYDION. This is all very creepy, my dear Timarion, and just hearing about it makes me shiver. But I have two questions. How on earth were you able to see the doorkeepers' faces if the darkness was so thick,[112] and how did you find out all the other things that you seem to have?

TIMARION. It is true, my dear Kydion, that everything in Hades is dark and sunless. The answer is, the people down there have artificial lights.[113] The common vulgar masses[114] use wood and coal fires and torches, whereas those who were men of quality on earth have lamps and live their lives under brilliant illumination. Indeed, I recognised a lot of them as I walked by their abodes and sampled their infernal hospitality.

KYDION. I see. But carry on, my friend, and bring the rest of your story back into proper sequence.[115]

TIMARION. Well, once I had been brought inside the iron gate, we were no longer transported through the air as before, nor did we carry on roaring and zooming as we had done through the upper world as though it had been enemy territory. No, we now began to walk, taking it easy, partly because of fatigue from the fast trip down but maybe also because my guides, pitiless though they were, felt sorry for me. As we journeyed along, we passed by many poor and humble habitations, and everyone everywhere came out to meet[116] the conductors of the dead or stood up in respect, like schoolboys for their masters.[117]

Next we came upon a lodging place bright with light. Beside it was lying some old man with a beard that wasn't all that long. He was reclining on his left elbow and was propping up the side of his face with his left hand. Alongside him reposed a large bronze pot full of salt pork and Phrygian cabbage, all drenched with fat.[118] The old man kept slowly inserting his

16

17

right hand into the pot, not using just two or three fingers but plucking the food out with his entire hand and guzzling it down greedily to the point of licking up what was running down his chin. He seemed by his expression to be a decent and congenial sort of person. Indeed, he was, for as we came close, he gave us a friendly and cheerful look, gazed at me quite calmly without turning a hair, and said, "Come and sit down beside me, stranger, dip in and make the most of a dead man's feast."

I declined, both because I had lost my various faculties thanks to the change of life I had undergone[119] and because I was afraid that my guides would give me a rival meal of knuckle sandwich. But they, in fact, were exchanging greetings with the dead as though back from a long journey and were quite engrossed in their friendly conversations, which gave me the opportunity to see what life among the dead was like. Whilst I was looking at this old man, somebody from the crowd, one of the great unwashed but quite respectable-looking in spite of that, accosted me and asked some very basic questions, such as who was I, where was I from, and by what sort of death had I been brought down to Hades? My answers were equally to the point, though truthful.

18   Since I was tied up with this character, I asked him who the old man was and what was his name. He had by now become quite affable towards me, and replied, "Ah, my new-found friend, don't ask what his name is. It's not safe for you to ask or me to answer because Aeacus and Minos have issued a very strict law against anyone who asks or discloses the old man's actual name. Under this legal constraint, that subject has fallen into the category of unmentionables. However, I will tell you everything that can legally be told about him. He comes from Great Phrygia,[120] so they say, of a noble and famous family. He lived a good life on earth, died in the richness of old age, and now, as you can see, lives in Hades on the fat of the land."[121]

That was his story. It made me roll my eyes, and, as I did so, I caught sight of two mice, big and fat and smooth, just like the pigs men rear at home[122] and feed on flour and bran. Gasping for breath at the strangeness of this sight, I turned to my companion and said, "My dear, good, friend, everything in Hades seems well and truly hateful and abominable, the sorts of things that in life particularly lend themselves to be cursed.[123] And these mice that you have here I find the most unbearable thing of all. To someone like me who loathes these creatures more than every other loathsome thing,[124] it seemed some sort of consolation to come down here, in that I would at least be rid of their troublesomeness.[125] But if I have to fight against them here as well, then I demand another death and another descent to a different Hades."

After a pause, my kind informant replied, "My friend, I am amazed at your ingenuousness and manifest ignorance of what is what. Don't you realise that all mice are earthborn and that they spring up from small cracks in the earth that occur in times of drought? Hence it is more logical that they should live underground and multiply in Hades, rather than up on earth in the land of the living. They don't come down to us from up there, they go up to the surface of the earth from our world down here. So you mustn't be astonished to find mice living here with us but should realise that they are our regular companions, unconcerned about the field mouse and her problems. Don't you see how glad they are to see this old man eating? Just look how happy they are, rattling their jaws and licking their lips, anticipating more of a fill of the fat than the old man."[126] I looked closely at the mice and saw that what he said was quite true. "Don't you see," he went on, "how they are heading for the old man's beard and are waiting for him to fall asleep? The minute they hear the snores he always comes out with when asleep, like a monster in a play,[127] they sneak out and nuzzle all around his chin, licking it quite clean of all the fatty broth and devouring every last crumb hanging down from it. That's where they live, and, as you can see for youself, that's how fat they get."

Thanks to the temporary preoccupation of my guides, I got the chance to find all this out. But then they came over to me, and we resumed our journey. When we had travelled about four stades,[128] passing by many habitations as we did so, we came to an

19

20

abode that was illuminated both by lamplight within and by a shining white tent.[129] A loud groaning was coming from this tent. I looked around and perceived that my guides were once again busy gossiping with the dead—friends and relations, this time, so it seemed—so I stole quietly up to the tent like a thief and peeked through the entrance flap to see what was inside and who it was making that deep and melancholic moaning.

Lying there on the ground was a man whose eyes had been gouged out with iron.[130] He was propped up on his left side and elbow, with a Spartan[131] rug spread out under him. He was a big-framed individual, sinewy rather than fleshy, with a broad chest.[132] In the words of the poet,[133] "He lay great in his greatness, forgetful of his horsemanship, resembling not a man that eats grain so much as a wooded peak."

Another old man[134] squatted beside him, trying to lighten the great burden of his suffering with conversation and words of encouragement. But he appeared not to want to listen, constantly shaking his head and pushing the old man away with his hand, whilst all the time poison kept oozing down from his mouth.[135]

21 When I had well and truly seen everything there, I began to look for a place from which I could keep an eye on my guides, constantly checking on them as I did so. The next thing I knew, I had bumped into one of the dead, an old and shrivelled-looking individual who had all the hallmarks of those whom wasting[136] fever brings to the grave. On seeing me, he perceived that I was newly dead from my colour, since those who have just come down to Hades retain a little of their earthly hue, thanks to which they are easily recognised as newcomers by the old-timers. He gave me a friendly greeting, "Welcome, freshman corpse,[137] tell me what's going on up there. How many mackerel can you get for an obol? What's the price of tunny, especially young tunny, and little sprats? What's the price of oil, wine, corn, all that stuff? Wait a minute, I missed out the most important thing of all. Was there a good catch of sardines? They were my favourite food up on earth, even more than pike."[138]

I gave him what Plato calls the whole truth in reply to each of his questions, and when I had filled him in on earthly news, I asked him in return to tell me who was the person living in that nearby tent, who the old man was squatting alongside him, and what was the reason for the groaning.

He replied civilly. "The person living in this tent, whose deep[139] groans you heard, is the famous Diogenes of Cappadocia.[140] You will have known the main facts about him when you were alive, how he was elevated to the throne, how he campaigned against the Eastern barbarians, and how he was taken prisoner. Then he was freed, but on returning to Constantinople, instead of being restored to his kingdom, he was overwhelmed by a revolt and by treachery, being blinded, as you can see, in spite of a treaty.[141] And as though all this were not enough, he was also afflicted with the agony of a terrible poison. The old man squatting by him is a noble from Great Phrygia.[142] The emperor made use of him on earth as councillor and partner in all that he did. So now, in pity for his misfortune and in memory of their former intimacy, he stays with his master all the time, trying as far as he can to alleviate the burden of his woes with suitable consolations and encouragements."

He was telling me all this when the guides came back over and started to drive me on more urgently, saying, "Get a move on, you're scheduled to meet the college of judges and be removed from our custody any moment now." "What," I asked, "don't tell me there are judges and lawsuits and judgements down here as well?" "Yes," they replied, "and more than that, down here a man's entire life is inspected point by point and he is judged accordingly for every single thing, and there can never be any appeal against the decision of the court of judges."

We got going on this note, but we had only got a short distance before we were accosted by a tall, white-haired man, shrivelled in body but otherwise elegant. He was certainly full of talk, for he puffed[143] out his cheeks as he spoke and roared with noisy laughter and called out a welcome to my guides, adding, "So, who's this new corpse you are taking along?" He then

22

23

turned his eyes on me, looked closely into my face, and gave me the once-over.[144] After a brief inspection, he called out loudly[145] and clearly, "By the good gods,[146] I know this man. It's Timarion, my dear young friend Timarion with whom I often had some fine dinners and who used to come to my lectures when I held the sophistic chair in Constantinople."[147] With this, he threw both his hands around me and gave me a hearty embrace.

I froze with shame at being thus received by a person of such obvious importance whilst I failed to recognise who it was who was welcoming me, having no idea who he was and so not knowing the correct form by which to reciprocate his greeting.[148]

He saw my quandary and got rid of it by anticipating the question. "My good sir, do you really not recognise Theodore of Smyrna,[149] the biggest[150] sophist, who gained fame in Constantinople from the declamation of solemn and distinguished discourses?" On hearing this, I was thunderstruck by the change in his face and figure, and replied, "Sir, I remember the voice and the brilliant lectures and the resonant delivery and the impressive size[151] that were the trademarks of that great sophist from Smyrna in life. But I cannot reconcile that man whose body was knotted up with arthritis and who had both to be carried in on a litter to declaim before the emperor and to eat propped up on his elbow with this radiant health and fit-looking body I see before me."[152]

24 The sophist replied, "I will relieve you of that puzzlement as well, my star pupil. In the life above, I gave many discourses that pleased Their Majesties, in return for which I earned many gold pieces[153] and enjoyed many unusual benefits. But I squandered everything on extravagant banquets and sybaritic dinners. Well, you must know yourself, since you were often invited to dine with me, that the money I spent on food rivalled that of any potentate. And that was the root cause of my arthritis and the stiffness in my fingers and the excessive buildup of phlegm that made my joints all plugged and stiffened up like stone.[154] The consequent agonies wore me out body and soul. My body became a useless burden to me. But everything is different down here. A philosopher's

life-style, plain food, a quiet life—carefree, that's it.[155] Best of all, I've calmed my raging stomach with a diet of cress, mallow, and asphodel[156] and have now reached Hesiod's[157] definition of true happiness: 'Nor know they how great is the refreshment of mallow and asphodel.'

"Let me tell you, in the life above it was verbal dexterity and crowd-pleasing[158] wit that counted. Down here, it is all philosophy and true culture, with less demagogic display. Right, now that I've told you all that, you need be confused no longer and can stop wondering as from this moment about what has happened to me, so that we can get back on our old terms. But not before you have reciprocated. I've told you everything, so you tell me what sort of death removed you from life, and what was the reason you came down to join us here."[159]

"There was no ordinary cause of death, best of masters,"   25
I replied. "No enemy's sword, no attack by bandits, no stroke of ill fortune, no long illness to exhaust my body. No, it was rather the abuse of authority on the part of these conductors of the dead to your abode who brutally snatched me from my body while I was still living. To give you a brief résumé[160] of what happened to me from beginning to end, I had been to Thessalonica for a particular reason and was planning to return home when I was struck down by a raging fever along with a serious inflammation of the liver. To top that, I had an unquenchable gastric flux. All my bile emptied out along with a little bit of blood on the surface that turned it red. I had constant dysentery all the way to the river Hebrus—you know that big river in Thrace that is deep enough for boats. We put up there for a while in a billet by the river, so that both I and the horses that were carrying me could get some rest. Spending the night there made me feel better, so I thought it would be a good idea to stay a second night there as well.

"So I did. Night came. Everyone was sound asleep, myself included. But in the very dead of the night,[161] when I was still in the land of dreams, these accursed devils appeared by my bed. On seeing them, I was struck dumb and couldn't wake up, and so with this apparition in my mind I was pulled out of my body. And the only so-called reason for my being carried away that I heard from them was these words: 'This is the man who has lost one of his elements, namely all his bile. But it has been decreed by Aesculapius and Hippocrates and the rest of the medical profession that anyone in such a condition shall not be allowed to go on living. Wherefore this wretch must be separated from his body.'

26   "That is what they said. And I, led by a force I cannot explain, was crumpled up inside myself like a tuft of wool and was simply blown out through my nostrils and mouth,[162] like the puffy breaths that are blown out when you yawn. And so, as you can see, I was brought down to Hades, or to put it poetically,[163] 'The soul flitting from the body came down to the underworld.' But if what those accursed academics say about destiny is true, I had not yet fulfilled my allotted span of life but was removed by force from my mortal clay. So now, if there really are in the lower world lawcourts and judgements that punish evil deeds,[164] I beg you to help me, your pupil, by bringing a charge of illegal procedure against these devils."

At this point I broke down and cried. But he was moved to pity and compassion by my distress and replied, "Cheer up, my good fellow, I will help you to the best of my abilities, and I can confidently promise that you will be returned to a second span of life and will have the resurrection you desire. In return, you must arrange to send down from up there what I most desire, namely some of my favourite foods."[165]

27   "I hope you are right," I said, "but, frankly, I'll believe it when it happens. For the outcome you so confidently predict seems as improbable, indeed as unrealistic, as the things sculptors and painters create in their studies, hippocentaurs, sphinxes, all the other mythological fabrications of the ancients. I really would like to know, prince of professors, on what you base your blithe promise to get me free, since the case will be judged by Aeacus and Minos,[166] who are pagan and so hostile to a Galilaean[167] like me; and you too are a disciple and alumnus of Christ."

The sophist replied, "You yourself ought to know the basis for my total optimism. I have a keenness of mind that can sharply combat any counterattack and that is quick to fasten on the appropriate response to any rival arguments. I also have a ready wit that knows how to come up with the killing epigram, a fluent and lucid style in general, and some medical jargon as well. Armed with all this, I shall find a *point d'appui,* however small, for my brief and shall wrestle these clever medical-type pagan gods to the ground.

"For Aesculapius,[168] thanks to his bad reputation and quack oracles, hasn't uttered a word these many years. Indeed, he has taken a veritable vow of silence. But if he is absolutely forced to by other people's questions, then the questioner is obliged to fashion his query in a way that is suitable for a yes or no answer, so that he can indicate his response simply by nodding or shaking his head. *That's* how Aesculapius will render his verdict.

"Hippocrates, if he speaks at all, won't say much, and what little he may come out with will be in words of one syllable or two at the most. And even those will be obscure, absurd aphorisms that are quite out of place in a court of law, for example, 'Prescribe and administer cooked things, not raw' and 'In the tumults and the vomitings of the belly,' absolute gibberish to the ears of judges who speak a different language.[169]

"Minos, you see, is a Cretan, and Aeacus is a genuine Greek from Thessaly in the Old World. So whenever any dead Ionian or Dorian attempts to address them, they immediately hoot and holler as though at a joke.

"Then there's Erasistratus,[170] but he's not only quite unversed in the sophistic arts, he's also devoid of the most basic training and isn't even a competent theoretician. He only acquired that meaningless, undeserved reputation[171] of his by constant plugging along, plus his natural savvy and various experiences. *That* was how he managed to diagnose Antiochus' love for Stratonice, which was the source of his meteoric rise to fame.[172]

"Best of all, the godlike Galen,[173] the one man I really do

28

29

fear, is, no doubt providentially, absent right now from the medical conclave. The reason is, so I heard from his own lips a little while ago, his book on the difference between fevers. He's presently tucked away in a corner,[174] far from all noise and bother, busy adding another revised appendix of material omitted from his first edition. Indeed, he once remarked that the revised version would be bigger than the first one. With him away, it will be an easy business for me to overcome these proud but not loud[175] medicals.

"And another thing, don't be afraid of the judges because they are pagan. For they are genuinely devoted to justice. It is precisely for that reason that they were elevated to the supreme court.[176] They aren't concerned about religious differences between themselves and the people who come before them. Everyone is allowed to stick to the religion of his choice.[177] Nevertheless, since the religion of the Galilaeans has spread all over the world, prevailing as it does in all of Europe and much of Asia, divine providence deemed it only fair that somebody of that persuasion should sit on the bench along with these pagan judges.[178] And so Theophilus, who once ruled over Byzantium, is the legal partner of the other two, and no decision of any sort can be put into effect without his consent. You will remember from the historians' accounts of him how completely devoted to justice he was.[179] So there is absolutely no reason to fear that we won't get a fair hearing or be deprived of due process. Well then, let's get ourselves down to the court. Only when we do, you'd better keep your mouth shut, since you are no good as a lawyer. I'll do all the talking."[180]

30   At that moment the guides came over and asked him if I was known to him. He confirmed that I was a student of his, adding, "I will come with you and help him to plead his case against you, since he has been so unjustly treated in being snatched away from life before his time."

On that note, we all set off together and continued on our way. When we had travelled a further fifteen stades or so through that dark and gloomy land, we eventually glimpsed a shaft of light shining in the distance. As we got closer, it became broader, and so little by little we were able to emerge from the darkness and find ourselves in a well-lighted oasis which had running water and was luxuriant with all kinds of plants, thanks to the irrigation provided by a very large river.[181]

There were groves of every kind, and sparrows singing very clearly and sweetly, all of this being on a bed of green turf. As I found out from the sophist, who was of course already an expert in things infernal, "Winter never touches the land, nor is there any change of season. Everything is indestructible and ageless, the trees bear fruit but never wither, the only season is spring that is eternally unchanging and unchanged."[182] From this description which the sophist gave me when we first began to see the shaft of light from afar, I realised that it was in fact the Elysian Fields and meadows of asphodel that are so famous on earth.

When we had reached the lighted spot, we sat down at the sophist's request and rested for a little while on the grass, after which we stood up and went on to take our places at the courtroom.

31

I felt very nervous, not knowing what went on there, and above all because I was quite incapable of pleading my own case, so I went up to the sophist and confided my fears to him. But he rallied my spirits with his experienced patter and assured me that everything would turn out for the best. "The only thing you have to concern yourself with," he remarked, "is making sure you send back those things I need from the upper world when you get back there. All the time I've been down here, I haven't been served a single bowl of broth enriched with pig's fat. You will get the complete list when your return to life has been confirmed by the court."

We kept walking and talking in this way until the court was, as they say, not a bowshot away, close enough in fact for us to hear the case that was just being concluded. It was Caesar's unjust murder by Brutus and Cassius.[183] What the outcome was, I cannot say, being too engrossed in my own problems to pay any close attention to anyone else's.

32   When they had stepped down, ushers of the court came up to us and asked, "How plead you, freshman corpse? You[184] shall now be summoned to the court." The sophist, elbowing me backwards, did all the talking: "Ministers of justice, take us directly to your most just leaders, whereupon you shall hear of the most impious and unlawful miscarriage of justice in recorded memory, namely the one wrought by these egregious corpse conductors upon this wretched client of mine. So pledging ourselves to be judged by you, O most upright of judges, in accordance with the laws of the dead, we now free ourselves of these wicked devils and invoke Minos and Aeacus and Theophilus the Byzantine against these accursed enemies of justice.[185]

"Seize them, I say, take them before the bench to be judged for their violation of the laws of the dead. For what law of Hades sanctions the snatching away of a soul from a body that is still living, from a man who, though sick, was clinging on to life on the back of a horse and who could eat an entire chicken in the course of a single day?"[186]

33   The ushers followed up this preamble by the sophist by laying hold of the conductors and leading them along with ourselves to the court, where we all stood before the seated figures of Aeacus and Minos and Theophilus the Galilaean.

The two Greek pagans wore flowing robes and turbans[187] on their heads like Arab chieftains. They also had on violet-coloured military boots. Theophilus, by contrast, wore nothing bright or shining. He was dressed in plain, simple black.[188] They say that when he was emperor he was similarly austere and inelegant in appearance. What he *did* shine in most splendidly was honest judgement and all the other virtues. Rough-looking as he was, he radiated gracefulness from his eyes, and in countenance he was shining[189] and confident.

At his shoulder stood a being dressed in white,[190] beardless like the eunuchs that attend empresses; he too shone brightly, and his face gave off radiance like the sun. He was continually whispering into the emperor's ear. Puzzled, I said to the sophist, "From what you told me a little while ago, I recognise this seated figure to be Theophilus of Byzantium. But I can't work out who this eunuch is."

"My dear Timarion," he replied, "don't you know that every Christian emperor has an angel to advise him on what he should do?[191] So this one is attending Theophilus here just as he did in life."

The ushers interrupted this exchange by hissing at us, whereupon the sophist puffed open his mouth in his usual style, solemnised his features, folded his hands, and boomed forth[192] with great clarity as follows:

"Timarion, son of Timonices, charges Oxybas and Nyktion, the conductors of the dead, with illegal procedure.[193] For the laws of the dead expressly state that no soul shall be brought down to Hades before the body is fatally damaged, either altogether or in one of its vital organs, and before it loses the vital energies of the spirit. What is more, even when the body has been separated from it, the soul must be allowed to remain near it for three days before the conductors are allowed to take it. But these devils, these body snatchers, conscientious and zealous beyond the call of duty as they are, came in the middle of the night[194] to my client's lodgings by the river, and, although he was still well and truly alive, in fact still eating and drinking and riding[195] his pack animal, they ripped his soul from his body though it clung on desperately and was hard to dislodge. Why, it has blood on it even now, and gobs of dried blood are peeling off it, so firmly rooted[196] in the body was it at the moment when it was so brutally separated. Gentlemen of the court, justice demands that my client be allowed to return to the upper world and recover his body and live out his appointed span. In due course, when his body and soul are separated through *natural* causes, he may then be brought back here and legitimately enlisted amongst the dead."

That was his opening speech. Minos looked fiercely[197] at the conductors and snapped, "Well, you scoundrels, let us hear your side of the story. It will not go well with you if you are proven to have transgressed the laws of the dead."

34

Nyktion, who was braver than Oxybas,[198] replied:

35   "Your most worshipful judges, we have had this responsibility since ancient times, indeed as far back as the reign of Chronos, hence we are very well acquainted with the proper procedures and we know all the right reasons for bringing a soul down to Hades.

"As for this poor devil Timarion, we had observed him in the process of losing through dysentery his fourth element all the way from Thessalonica to the greatest[199] river in Thrace. Acquainted as we are with the law laid down by the greatest medical brains to the effect that no man shall violate the law of nature by living on the basis of three elements, when we saw all his bile emptied out over a space of thirty days, we went to his bed and summoned forth his soul, since it was not lawful for it to remain in a body so deprived. But, your most worshipful judges, it is for you to render your verdict; we will submit ourselves to the law."

This was their defence.[200] The judges whispered amongst themselves for a little while before announcing that the sentence would be deferred for that day. "We need," they said, "the presence of the great doctors Aesculapius and Hippocrates so that we may reach the best possible verdict in concert with them. This is a case that calls for expert medical knowledge. Therefore, let the court stand adjourned. We shall meet with the great doctors in three days' time and clarify the point at issue."

After this proclamation, the judges rose and retired to a spot deeper within the meadow. The ushers took us along with the conductors towards the realm of darkness, not too far inside it though, but to where it bordered on the light, giving the effect of a kind of twilight zone[201] where the two regions met.

36   Even while the judges were still deliberating over what to do, the sophist had bent down and whispered into my ear, "You go to that pine (pointing out a tall and luxuriant one), and in its shade you will find various kinds of vegetables, some familiar to you, others not. Pluck them up by the roots and bring them back with you. There is nothing there that is

poisonous;[202] they are all nice and nourishing. And if you happen to have any left over, be so kind as to share them with me. The things that grow here have the advantage of a heavenly breeze and air, hence they produce a sweet scent before you eat them and just as sweet a burping afterwards."

My master didn't have much trouble persuading me. I went to the pine tree, collected as many vegetables[203] as seemed decent, and loaded up a good supply. Upon rejoining the sophist, we at once moved off with our guides and their adversaries. And so we spent two days and nights in the twilight zone. Around cockcrow, as you might put it, on the third day, we got up and set off for the court. By moving fast, we got to the judges' bench before anyone else.

Presently, to quote Homer again,[204] "Saffron-robed Dawn spread all over the earth," disclosing the figures of Aesculapius and Hippocrates taking their seats along with the judges to join in the proceedings. They began to consider what their verdict should be in our case and ordered the clerk of the court to acquaint them with the minutes of the hearing held in respect of Nyktion and Oxybas three days ago. The clerk proclaimed in formal legalese, "Let those persons who brought the prior indictment against Oxybas and Nyktion, the conductors, three[205] days before the present one present themselves forthwith, that this most worshipful court may adjudge and pronounce its sentence this very day."

The ushers nudged all of us forward, plaintiffs and defendants alike, to stand in front of the bench. Whilst the sophist concentrated his attention on our brief, I concentrated mine on the appearance of Aesculapius and Hippocrates. I wasn't able to see Aesculapius' face properly because it was covered by a gold-spangled veil which was also diaphanous and transparent in such a way that he, poor fool that he was with his pathetic belief in his own divinity, could see everything but could be seen by no one. Hippocrates, by contrast, looked like some Arab with his tall and pointed[206] turban for headgear. He wore a cloak that reached his feet and that was unbelted and totally seamless, without any openings or apertures. His beard was

37

flowing and grizzled, his hair was closely cropped[207] to the very skin, Stoic-style—indeed, for all I know, it was from him that Zeno got the idea of short hair for himself and his followers.

While I was taking all this in, the clerk produced the court record and read the minutes out aloud: Timarion, son of Timonices, prosecuting Oxybas and Nyktion, etc., etc., the whole story right down to the judges' deliberation and decision to defer sentence until Hippocrates and Aesculapius should be available to offer their expert opinions. When the clerk had finished his reading of the record, Hippocrates and Aesculapius whispered together for a little while,[208] then they summoned Erasistratus to join them, which led to another short pause. After all that, Hippocrates flashed a fierce look and said, "Nyktion and Oxybas, tell us without any prevarication from what disease Timarion's soul was suffering and whether it was actually separated from his body when you brought it down here or whether you snatched it away by force when it was still clinging on."

38 Pausing briefly to gather their wits, the conductors responded,[209] "Greatest of the physicians, we have in no way disobeyed or dishonoured your regulations. After all, it was you and your colleagues on earth who established the hard and fast rule that no one should keep on living or breathing who was not fully comprised of the four elements—blood, phlegm, black bile, yellow bile—and that whoever happened to be deprived of one of these four should under no circumstances be allowed to live on.

"Therefore, in fulfillment of our allotted duty in the upper world, on seeing this poor wretch continuously coughing up bile mixed with blood for thirty days and nights, we perceived on the basis of our medical expertise that he could not be allowed to live any longer. We ask you, how could he possibly have had any of this elemental humour left in him after coughing it up in such quantities for so many days? You may then rest assured that we had no need to use force to separate his soul from his body. Quite the contrary, we went in gently through the nostrils and drew it up[210] with a light sucking ac-tion. It put up no resistance, since his body was by that time completely exhausted from its continuous secretions."

After offering this defence, the conductors fell silent. The ushers turned to us and said, "Now you give us your side of the story and quickly, so that the divine Aesculapius, the superphysician, may take his leave of the court, since for many years now, in fact ever since he was awarded divine status, he has avoided contact with mortals as much as possible."

At this, the sophist puffed open his mouth[211] and spoke as follows:

"Your Honours, and you, too, presidents and executive members of the medical association, you have just heard the babbling excuses of these accursed devils and the pathetic and illogical pretence of an argument they have attempted to string together.[212] Now, in rebuttal, I shall show how they have hoisted themselves with their own petard."

Hippocrates meanwhile had turned round and whispered into the ear of one of the ushers, asking who and from where was this loud and wordy[213] advocate of Timarion. The usher filled him in on all the details:[214] originally from Smyrna, he had been brought up in Constantinople, where he was appointed to the chair of sophistry and where he filled the palace with his audacity, earning in the process enormous honour and patronage from Their Majesties. That's what I heard the usher tell Hippocrates as I listened in for a little while.

The sophist was going on, "That my client's body was not yet ready for death is something that the conductors themselves will have fully to acknowledge. I ask you, how could this body, travelling as it was on horseback from Thessalonica, possibly be described as ready for death and unfit to go on living? Moreover, it is a basic principle of funerals that even when the soul is separated, it shall only be brought down to Hades *after* the due rituals have been performed. This principle holds good for all religions,[215] each of which have their own special customs. In the case of the Christians, these rites are performed on the third, ninth, and fortieth days.[216] Yet these creatures brought my client's soul down to Hades without waiting for them."

Nyktion broke in on this point with a loud protest, "But there was no one there to perform the rites for Timarion. He was a stranger in a foreign land and had nobody who could perform the rites for him. . . ."[217]

"But to settle the issue of whether or not you snatched away this soul by force, let its condition be examined by some officials with good eyesight.[218] For if it is the case that it was snatched away by force, there will still be bits of flesh sticking to it."

40 Two officials called Oxyderkion and Nyktoleustes[219] were immediately detailed to make the inspection. When they had made a thorough investigation of the condition of the soul, they reported back to the judges as follows: "External examination shows the entire soul to be defiled by gore, of a colour commonly found on men who fall in battle, the result of sweat mixing with blood.[220] But our detailed internal investigation discloses that some parts of the soul are still suffused with pure blood and still emit some particle of living breath. Furthermore, some pieces of flesh *are* stuck to it, containing blood and the essence of life."

At this news, the sophist bawled, "There you have it, gentlemen, the vindication of my own argument. For if the soul was still managing to cling obstinately to the body, how could its fourth element have been entirely drained away? According to the theories of the most distinguished doctors, nature surrenders a soul without a struggle when it actually has lost an element. But in this case, it was not the element itself that was voided, but rather the food ingested every day was forcibly expelled when turned into a secretion that was bile-like but not real bile, as a result of the inflammation of the liver. This is quite clear from the results of the second examination. That part of the soul of Timarion which was near to the liver when the bleeding began is all rendered down into bile. And, organically speaking, it is precisely there that our daily intake of food, once transformed into a bile-like substance, produces and gets rid of our bodily refuse which is equally bile-like. There can be only one conclusion. What was secreted was not pure elemental bile but ordinary bodily wastes that are voided along with bile, more than usual in this particular case because of the inflamed condition of the liver."

When the sophist had finished his peroration, silence was proclaimed in the courtroom. After a brief pause, the judges discussed the evidence amongst themselves and in consultation with medical experts. Then they cast their votes in the usual lots.[221] The verdict was in our favour.

A writing tablet was produced, and none other than the Byzantine Professor took up his position. The ushers[222] told me that he had been appointed chief officer of the court on account of his skill and speed in improvisation. "Look," they said, "you will see how short a time it will take him to dictate the verdict to the clerk of the court."

After retiring briefly the judges summoned the Byzantine Professor, who was accompanied by Aristarchus,[223] and spelled out to him all the detailed provisions of the judgement. The Byzantine Professor made the announcement without any hesitation, although he whispered[224] most of it, being unable to force out the words clearly through the crookedness of his lips.[225] Aristarchus acted as the clerk, Phrynichus[226] as the presiding official.[227] When the entire text of the decision had been dictated to the clerk, he read it out to the entire assembly. It went like this:

"It has been resolved by this most worshipful college of great physicians, not forgetting the divine Aesculapius, that Nyktion and Oxybas, in so much as they have transgressed against the laws of the dead, shall be removed forthwith from their office of conductors of souls, and that Timarion shall be restored to life and live in his own body.[228] In due time, when he has completed his allotted span, and has had the holy rituals performed over him, then and only then shall he be brought back down to Hades by the legally appointed conductors of the dead."

With that, the reading came to an end, the judges stood up, and the court was adjourned. The judges themselves retired to their usual place in the meadow whilst Aesculapius moved off more slowly along with the doctors to another spot therein.

The Christians for their part all shouted and jumped for joy and congratulated the sophist from Smyrna, praising him to the skies for the arguments and techniques and methods of his speech.

The ushers, who had been given the job of returning me to the upper world, took me by the hand and began to escort me back through Hades. And as we made our way through the dark regions of the underworld, we came upon the area where the philosophers and sophists lived. My sophist, tired both from the journey and from his intense mental concentration, asked the ushers to let us stay the night with this assembly of great minds. The next day (he suggested), we could take our leave of him, since he intended to stay with them, and so get back to life all the more quickly.

We agreed. Then, in the words of the poet,[229] "The other gods and horse-equipped men slept through the night, but sweet slumber touched me not." For wanting to find out as much as I possibly could about Hades, I stayed awake all through the night, giving everything the onceover.

43   I saw Parmenides, Pythagoras, Melissus, Anaxagoras, Thales, and the other founders of the philosophical schools sitting quietly together and discussing their respective beliefs[230] very calmly and unemotionally. The one thing they did agree on was their loathing of Diogenes,[231] whom they had excluded from their circle. He was pacing up and down, not squatting on his haunches, and in his usual fierce and combative style was trying to provoke everybody else to an argument.

I also saw John Italus[232] trying to sit down alongside Pythagoras, but the latter rejected him brusquely, saying, "You filthy rat, you who have put on the mantle of the Galilaeans which they call divine and heavenly, meaning baptism, where do you get the nerve to join us, men who spent their lives in epistemology and syllogistic thought? Either take off that strange robe or take yourself off right away from our company." But John Italus wouldn't take it off.

He was followed by a mannikin or half-man,[233] a slavish
fellow, to be more accurate, a city type, very ribald and
coarse, who abused everyone he met in iambic verse, a character quite devoid of intelligence but one who could deceive
the ignorant mob with his promises, promises line. You only
had to exchange a word or two with him to realise that there
was nothing decent or clever about him. He seemed to be
nothing more than a clone of his own teacher, a malignant,
abusive, fickle, conceited son of a bitch who was everything
you would expect such qualities to produce.[234]

But he really caught a Tartar[235] this time. For he went up   44
to Diogenes the Cynic and arrogantly tried to buttonhole him.
Diogenes, though, who had recently increased his own stock of
shamelessness,[236] was not to be caught like that. To show his
contempt for his opponent's brand of offensiveness, he snorted
and howled like a dog that is always barking. That provoked
John, who was also an amateur of Cynic dogma,[237] to start
howling in his turn. This all ended in a wrestling match. The
Italian got hold of Diogenes in the shoulder with his teeth,[238]
but Diogenes countered by fastening his onto his rival's throat
and probably would have throttled him, had not Cato the
Roman,[239] who didn't care much for philosophers, extricated
John from Diogenes' mouth.

"You dirty rat," snarled Diogenes. "Why, no less a person
than Alexander, son of Philip, the one who conquered all of
Asia so easily, came to me in Corinth while I was sunbathing,
and *he* spoke to me in tones of respect and humility. So where
do you get the nerve to treat me as an inferior, you of all
people, whom the Byzantines treated as scum and who was
hated by all the Galilaeans? By the Cynic philosophy,[240] of
which sect I am the leader, if you dare to say as much as one
more word to me, you will get a second painful death and
burial."

Cato took John by the hand and led him a safe distance
away. But when they trespassed upon the territory of the
dialecticians,[241] the latter rose as one man and pelted John
with stones, shouting, "Get him out of here, Cato. A *dumm-*

kopf who failed grammar in life and who was a laughingstock when he tried to write speeches doesn't belong here."

So John, ridiculed and abused by all, retreated groaning, "Aristotle, Aristotle,[242] O syllogism, O sophism, where are you now that I need you? If only you had been here to help me, I could have wiped the floor with these idiot philosophers and this pig-dealing[243] bag of wind,[244] Diogenes."

45   This scene was interrupted by the arrival of the Byzantine Professor himself. The philosophers greeted him graciously as he drew near to them, and there was much calling out of "Hail, Byzantine." But for all that, he had to talk to them standing up, for they made no move to offer him a seat, and he didn't venture to take one uninvited.[245] When he went over to the sophists, though, it was a very different story. They rose as one man in his honour and gave him an enthusiastic welcome. He got the option of sitting down in the middle of their circle if he wanted to relax, or towering over them all in the chair which they offered him as the reward for the gracefulness of his eloquence, the charm and clarity of his diction, his affability, his gift of instant extemporisation, his natural skill in every literary genre.[246] They kept hailing him as "Sun King," which on enquiry I discovered was an allusion to a speech he had composed in the emperor's honour.[247]

KYDION.   Yes, yes, Timarion, but aren't you also going to fill me in on what sort of reception your own Smyrnite sophist got from that professorial assembly?

TIMARION.   Well, Kydion, as I was about to say, he kept himself largely aloof from those sharp-witted leaders of the philosophical sects, except when he needed to ask a question or request clarification concerning a particular theory. But he got on like a house on fire with the rhetoricians, especially Polemo and Herodes and Aristides.[248] They were men he could approach with confidence, since they were his compatriots. And they in their turn put him in their midst as soon as they met, and they began to pick his brains on points of rhetorical arrangement and style and delineation of character.

So, my friend, this is what I saw as I rested throughout the   46
summery night from dusk to dawn along with the usher and
the sophist,[249] although they slept all this time that I was keeping watch. When they woke up, the sophist immediately came
over to me and said, "Get up, Timarion, my boy, and get on
your way back up to life. It's a long time since anyone was
resurrected.[250] But don't forget to send me the things I want so
badly from up there."[251] "Everything I have shall be yours, I
promise you," I replied, "but you had better spell out exactly
what it is you want so that I can take care of your wants. So,
give me the details."

"My boy, please send me a five-month-old lamb, two three-
year-old hens that have been fattened and slaughtered, the
kind the poulterers[252] sell in the market, I mean the kind that
good butchers have removed the stomach fat from and laid it
across their thighs on the outside, and a one-month-old sucking pig and a nice fat and fleshy sow's belly."[253]

When he had given me this list, the sophist embraced me in
a fond farewell, adding, "Bon Voyage back to life, but go
quickly so that your nearest and dearest will know you are safe
before the news of your death gets to Constantinople and your
relatives and friends start mourning. For I know that, as the
poet[254] puts it, there are many who love you."

So we parted. I began my journey at once and did not stop
for any reason. On the way, I saw on the left-hand side of the
road Philaretus of Armenia, Alexander of Pherae, and Nero,
the worst of them all, shovelling human excrement so noxious
that a whiff of it penetrated as far as the road.[255] Finally, I
reached the opening, and with the usher behind me and no
one trying to block me this time, I went up through it[256] right
away into the air, where I saw the Pleiades and the Bear.

By myself I would not have known which way to go to   47
find my body, but I was transported through the air as though
blown by the wind until I came to the river and recognised the
house in which my body was lying. I said good-bye to the
usher on the river bank, left him there, and went in through
the opening in the roof which had been specially contrived to

release smoke from the hearth.[257] I found my body and reentered it through the nostrils and mouth. A combination of the frosty winter weather and *rigor mortis* had made it very cold. All that night I felt as though I had a bad chill. But the next day I was able to pack my bags and set out for Constantinople.

And here I am, my dear Kydion, safe and sound. You've heard the whole story now.[258] Do me a favour and look out for some new corpses to which we can give the things the sophist ordered and send them down to him. Only it mustn't be any respectable[259] class of person who might resent the job but rather one of those filthy Paphlagonians from the market who will see a profit for himself in being sent down to Hades with some pork. Meanwhile, my inquisitive friend, it's bedtime, so let us say good-bye and go our separate ways home.

ABBREVIATIONS

AB	*Analecta Bollandiana*
AC	*Acta Classica*
B	*Byzantion*
BCH	*Bulletin de correspondance héllénique*
BF	*Byzantinische Forschungen*
BHM	*Bulletin of the History of Medicine*
BMGS	*Byzantine and Modern Greek Studies*
BS	*Byzantinoslavica*
BZ	*Byzantinische Zeitschrift*
Byz. St.	*Byzantine Studies*
CR	*Classical Review*
DOP	*Dumbarton Oaks Papers*
Ducange	C. Du Fresne Ducange, *Glossarium ad Scriptores Mediae et Infimae Graecitatis* (Leiden, 1688)
EEBS	*Epeteris Etereias Byzantinon Spoudon* (in Greek)
GIF	*Giornale italiano di filologia*
GRBS	*Greek, Roman and Byzantine Studies*
HSCP	*Harvard Studies in Classical Philology*
IRAIC	*Izvestiya Russkago Archeologischeskago Instituta v Konstantinopole*
JHS	*Journal of Hellenic Studies*
JOB	*Jahrbuch der österreichischen Byzantinistik*
JRS	*Journal of Roman Studies*
Lampe	G. W. Lampe, *A Patristic Greek Lexicon* (Oxford, 1969)
LSJ	H. G. Liddell, R. Scott, and H. Stuart Jones, *A Greek-English Lexicon,* 9th ed. (Oxford, 1940); *Supplement,* ed. E. A. Barber (Oxford, 1968)
MGHAA	*Monumenta Germanicae Historiae Auctorum Antiquissimorum* (Berlin, 1897–1919)
NJKA	*Neue Jahrbuch für das klassische Altertumwissenschaft*
PG	Migne, *Patrologia Graeca*
PMGM	J. L. Ideler, ed., *Physici et Medici Graeci Minores* (Berlin, 1841)
PP	*Past and Present*

Abbreviations

REA	*Revue des études arméniennes*
RESE	*Revue des études sud-est européennes*
SAMN	*Society for Ancient Medicine Newsletter*
Sophocles	E.A. Sophocles, *Greek Lexicon of the Roman and Byzantine Periods* (Cambridge, Mass., 1887)
Stephanus	H. Stephanus, *Thesaurus Graecae Linguae* (Paris ed., 1831–65)
TAPA	*Transactions of the American Philological Association*
TAPhilS	*Transactions of the American Philosophical Society*
VVrem	*Vizantijskij Vremennik*
WS	*Wiener Studien*
YCS	*Yale Classical Studies*

NOTES

NOTES TO INTRODUCTION

1. See for instance Browning, *Byzantina/Metabyzantina* 1 (1978), 121; Hussey, *Church and Learning in the Byzantine Empire 867–1185,* 111–2; Kazhdan, *BZ* 71 (1978), 311; Krumbacher, *Geschichte der byzantinischen Litteratur,* 467; Tozer, *JHS* 2 (1881), 235; Vasiliev, *History of the Byzantine Empire,* 497; Vyronis, *The Byzantine Saint,* 202; Wilson 111.
2. Cheetham, *Mediaeval Greece,* 198.
3. Kyriakis, *Byzantina* 5 (1973), 291.
4. Constantelos, *Byzantine Philanthropy and Social Welfare,* 60.
5. His unpublished treatise in Cod. Vindob. theol. 134 (Nessel) fol. 238–62 is entitled *Epitome of the Views of the Ancients on Nature and Physical Causes;* cf. Beck, *Kirche und theologische Literatur im byzantinischen Reich,* 616–7.
6. Romano's notion is founded on Browning, *B* 31 (1961), 229–36, albeit Browning himself did not adduce the *Timarion.*
7. Cf. Ostrogorsky 388 for the reference in the historian Nicetas Choniates to the "Petcheneg Holiday" still celebrated at the end of the 12th century to mark the Byzantine victory.
8. Dräseke, *NJKA* 29 (1912), 353; Vasiliev, *History of the Byzantine Empire,* 497.
9. Hunger 61–63.
10. Romano's edition 26–31, also argued in his other publications listed in the bibliography; his theory develops some remarks of Poliakova, Telenkov, and Lipsic, *VVrem* 6 (1953), 357–65.
11. E.g. Browning, *Byzantina/Metabyzantina* 1 (1978), 121; Garzya, *EEBS* 39–40 (1972–3), 344, n. 3; Kazhdan, *BZ* 71 (1978), 311; Macleod, *JHS* 96 (1976), 271; Vyronis, *The Byzantine Saint,* 202, n. 30.

12. Two examples are Eustathius, *Capture of Thessalonica* 86. 29, who calls George Palaeologus by the Homeric epithet *teichesipletes* ("stormer of cities"), and Constantine Manasses, *Hodoiporikon* 2. 57 f. For others, cf. Polemis, *The Doukai,* 12–15.

13. Following the earlier editor of Nicolas Callicles' poems, Sternbach 372; cf. the review of Romano's own edition by Leroy-Molinghen, *B* 52 (1982), 490.

14. Ed. Hesseling-Pernot 416.

15. *Praise of Heraclius* 1. 97–98; cf. Shahid, *DOP* 34–35 (1980–1), 255–7.

16. Buckler, *Anna Comnena,* 278 thinks Anna approved of Callicles because of his verses.

17. Except in *The Solecist,* but the authenticity of this dialogue is much debated; cf. Macleod's discussion in vol. 8 of his Loeb edition.

18. Cf. Browning, *B* 32 (1962), 181–4; Garzya, *RESE* 8 (1970), 611–21.

19. Cf. Browning, *B* 32 (1962), 194–7; *id. Byzantinobulgarica* 1 (1962), 279–97; Treu, *BZ* 4 (1895), 1–22. Michael's correspondence was edited by Cramer, who did not know whose it was, and more recently in the Budé series by Gautier (Paris, 1972).

20. Ed. Papadimitriu 321–4.

21. Ed. Horna.

22. Here following Karlsson, *Idéologie et cérémonial dans l'epistolographie byzantine,* 62–67.

NOTES TO TRANSLATION

Apart from acknowledged quotations of classical writers, the *Timarion* is a typically Byzantine cento of parodies, echoes, and borrowings from many sources. Some of these are of no interest to the Greekless reader, and are of little importance in themselves. Hence I have not cluttered up the notes with references to them; Romano gives most of them in his edition. My priorities were to include and discuss those passages which illuminate both the author's literary techniques and the general Byzantine knowledge and appreciation of the classics, and to include references to sources and parallels (certain or probable) missed by Romano.

1. This opening is also employed by Lucian, *Lexiphanes* 1, who in turn takes it from the beginning of Plato, *Hippias major* 281a, where there is the same motif of lateness being rebuked.

2. Timarion is either the author's real name, as proposed by Dräseke with the powerful support of Vasiliev (cf. the Introduction), or one made up along the lines of Plato's *Timaeus*, Lucian's *Timon*, or Psellus' *Timotheus*. The suffix *-arion* often has an endearing or diminutive force; cf. the *andrarion* ("mannequin") in ch. 43. The only examples of Timarion (his interlocutor Kydion is unattested) in Pape-Benseler, *Griechische Eigennamen,* are from four poems in the *Greek Anthology* by the Hellenistic epigrammatist Meleager: 5. 96, 204 (a female prostitute); 12. 109, 113 (a boy lover). Neither name is exemplified in Kirchner, *Prosopographia Attica.*

3. The quotation is from Homer, *Od.* 16. 23 (repeated at 17. 41), albeit in Kydion's version the first word is a grammatically vulgar, indeed hardly metrical, variant. The author is not likely to have made such a mistake. It may be either a scribal error or a subtle way of pointing up the relative ignorance of Kydion.

4. From Homer, *Il.* 16. 19, not 1. 163 via Lucian, *Zeus Rants* 1, as Romano says. For a similar opening flood of quotations, compare Lucian, *Menippus or The Descent into Hell* l.f., in the same context of a return from the underworld, though notice it is there the narrator, not the interlocutor, who thus begins.

5. The joke is apparently that Timarion has been away so long that he now seems as much a stranger as an old friend. The passages cited by Romano from Lucian and Psellus are irrelevant.

6. See the opening sections of Lucian's *Menippus or The Descent into Hell* for this same combination of Homer and Euripides, a parallel unnoticed by Romano.

7. Romano does not make it clear that this is a *parody* of Euripides, *Medea* 1317, nor that the author's version

derives from the novelist Heliodorus, *Ethiopica* 1. 8. That he did take it from Heliodorus is a fair presumption since the Homeric tag (*Od.* 9. 39) immediately following is also in the novelist (2. 21). For the many Byzantine testimonia to Heliodorus, including the critique by Psellus, cf. the edition of A. Colonna (Rome, 1938), 361–72. The Euripidean verse was parodied by Aristophanes, *Clouds* 1397, and was pastiched by the 11th- or 12th-century cento *Christus Patiens* 121, 437. Overall, this is a good example of how Byzantine literature can throw light on to classical texts; Page's otherwise excellent note in his edition of the *Medea* (Oxford, 1938) was unaware of the *Timarion*.

8. *Orestes* 1–3, without linguistic parody as in Lucian, *Zeus Rants* 1 (adduced by Romano), who varies the end of line 2. The lines were a popular tag in the author's time, being quoted in Theodore Prodromos' satire *Sale of the Lives* (p. 142, ed. La Porte du Theil), as well as by Anna Comnena 15. 2 on the subject of her own misfortunes; Romano does not notice the latter passage. The lines indeed had always had an impact. Cicero, *Tusculan Disputations* 4. 29. 63, translates them into Latin to give point to his anecdote that, at the play's première, Socrates had called for an encore of them.

9. This quotation conflates Homer, *Il.* 17. 446 with *Od.* 18. 130.

10. Kydion constantly indulges in this kind of self-defeating interruption, which results in the opening sections of the dialogue being the most spun out and least entertaining of all. To some extent, the technique is copied from Lucian who, however, was sensible enough not to allow a dramatic "feed" or stooge to talk too much.

11. Romano does not notice that Kydion's last three words echo Lucian, *Zeus Rants* 41. For the preceding phrase he adduces Homer, *Od.* 21. 249, though the author's version is in fact very free.

12. The Greek word is *pronoia*, which may in this context be a pun, since in Byzantine Greek it can mean amongst other things "provisions"; cf. Buckler, *Anna Comnena*, 496, n. 9.

13. Plain clothing traditionally suggested a man of virtue; cf. ch. 33 for the ostentatious austerity of emperor Theophilus. Psellus uses the same sartorial yardstick to judge emperors in his *Chronography*.

14. A reminder (one of several in the *Timarion*) of the dangers of travel in ancient and mediaeval times; cf. Casson, *Travel in the Ancient World;* Labage, *Medieval Travellers: The Rich and Restless*. That the *Timarion* may in part be a parody of travel literature can be seen from a collation of it with the *Hodoiporikon* of Constantine Manasses, a verse account of the author's pilgrimage to the Holy Land c. 1160, ed. Horna, *BZ* 13 (1904), 313–55. Notable common features include a graphic account of a terrible illness en route, with concomitant scorn of doctors, and extravagant praise of a member of the Ducas family. The appropriate parallels will be drawn in subsequent notes.

15. For the Byzantine concept of hospitality, modelled partly on classical ideals, partly on Christian, see Constantelos, *Byzantine Philanthropy and Social Welfare*, esp. 203–21.

16. The nuance may be a touch ambivalent here, since one of the Greek adjectives is *tyrannikos*, which usually has a bad sense, as later in ch. 24. Cf. ch. 44, where Alexander the Great is said to enslave (*douloo*) Asia, which looks odd from the Hellenic point of view, though it may simply be said to reflect the hostility of Diogenes.

17. Is this a joke at the expense of unworldly philosophers (absentminded professors, as we might call them) who fail to take the most elementary of alimentary precautions? Or is Timarion to be seen as a freeloader, the typical parasite of classical comedy?

18. Melodramatic exaggeration of tourist adventures (justified in Timarion's case) is common to all ages. For a criticism of it in the case of the 5th-century poet-historian-diplomat Olympiodorus of Thebes, see Photius, *Bibliotheca*, cod. 80, fr. 15 (using the verb *ektragodein*). Our author may have in mind Lucian's *Lover of Lies,* which contains some good jokes on the theme.

19. As earlier observed, it is Kydion who is exasperating with his inane interruptions.

20. "Scythian" is a typical Byzantine archaism, an affectation going back to the Greek historians of the 4th and 5th centuries A.D.; cf. Averil Cameron, *Agathias,* 82. Here it probably denotes the Petchenegs (or Patzinaks) of South Russia and may allude either to their defeat by Alexius I at Mt. Levunion on April 29, 1091, or to that inflicted on them in 1122 by John II Comnenus. If we could be sure that this equation is correct, their mention might furnish a clue to the date of the *Timarion;* cf. the Introduction.

21. Surely a conscious echo of the famous opening of Plato's *Republic* (the Greek has a verb of similar form and identical meaning as well as the identical preposition, also in the context of visiting a festival), though Romano does not compare the two passages, nor does Wilson.

22. The author uses a rare epithet (*peripuston*), no doubt to enhance the glory of Thessalonica. Anna Comnena 12. 4 tells of a visit to the Demetrius festival by her royal father. In spite of Kazhdan, *BZ* 71 (1978), 311, the author's description is not entirely dissimilar from that of Cameniates, especially his account of the church and choirs of St Demetrius. His praise of Thessalonica also belies Kazhdan's strange claim that the encomium of a city was a genre unknown to Byzantine literature before the 13th century. *Patria,* as such exercises were called, were frequent in prose and verse from the very beginnings of Byzantine literature; cf. Alan Cameron, *Historia* 14 (1965), 471–509. According to Eustathius, it was the mark of an historian to preface his account of a city's downfall with an "entertaining" description of it, whereas chroniclers of contemporary events eschew such flourishes.

23. Thessalonica, modern Saloniki, was the second most important city in the Byzantine empire after Constantinople. In the late Roman period it had been the seat of the prefect of Illyricum, thus foreshadowing the glory of its governor in the *Timarion* (ch. 7 f.). At some time in the 9th century it was elevated to the rank of theme (military zone); cf. Ostrogorsky, *History of the Byzantine State,* 194, n. 4, rather than Romano's note, which is spuriously

precise on the date and which misrepresents the views of Dvornik, *La vie de Saint Grégoire le Décapolite,* 36, 61–63. The city's contributions to the classical tradition, considerable at this period, will have been at least partly the result of its largely Greek population, in contrast to the Slavic nature of the neighbouring Strymon area; cf. the demographic study of Laiou-Thomadakis, *Peasant Society in the Late Byzantine Empire,* 80. Despite the protection of St Demetrius, whose miraculous interventions frequently saved his city against Slav attacks in the 7th to 9th centuries, the city fell to the Arabs in 904 and again to the Normans in 1185, thereby anticipating the fate of Constantinople herself in 1204. We possess the eyewitness account of this disaster by the famous churchman and scholar Eustathius, ed. S. Kyriakidis (Palermo, 1961). It is a reasonable presumption that the *Timarion* was written before the brutal sack of 1185, although the Byzantine capacity for ignoring contemporary events should not be forgotten; cf. Mango, *PP* 80 (1975), 3–18. Elaborating on this point in *Byzantium: The Empire of New Rome,* 241, Mango points out (to take the most pertinent of his several examples) that the aforementioned Lament over Thessalonica by Cameniates is datable not just after 904, the traditional view, but in the 15th century; cf. Kazhdan, *BZ* 71 (1978), 301–14. The same problems afflict Byzantine satires other than the *Timarion:* witness the *Philopatris,* a pseudo-Lucianic piece that has been variously dated from the 4th to the 11th century; cf. Baldwin, *YCS* 27 (1982). In the vicissitudes of Byzantine history between 1204 and 1453, Thessalonica was attacked and taken many times, ultimately falling to the Ottomans in 1430 after being handed over to the Venetians for protection in 1423 by its ruler Andronicus, son of Manuel II.

24. Celebrated to this day on October 26 by the Greek Orthodox Church. Demetrius was a high official martyred for his Christian faith in the last persecution under Diocletian and the Tetrarchy, A.D. 303–11. He was particularly associated with Sirmium, and was moved with the capital of the prefecture to Thessalonica in 442–3. In the

process, he was transformed from deacon to military saint, and also acquired the title *myrobletes* because of the emissions of holy oil from his tomb. His miraculous interventions on behalf of the city were mainly between the 7th and 9th centuries against the Slavs; a good example is that in the siege of 602, recorded in the *Miracles of St Demetrius* 1. 10 (*PG* 116. 1261 f.). As observed in the previous note, he was markedly less successful in the later period. In the present context, it is interesting that he should first appear on coins in the reign of Alexius I; cf. Hendy, *Coinage and Money in the Byzantine Empire 1081–1261,* 437. The church described in the *Timarion* was the third to be built, its predecessors having succumbed to fire and invasion. In 1430, the Turks converted it into the Mosque of Bajazet II. There is still much to be seen, despite severe fire damage in 1917. Since some of the above details are debatable, and also because the history of Demetrius and his cult is a good example for many aspects of the Byzantine religious temperament, readers should compare and contrast the studies of Cormack, Delehaye, Lemerle, Runciman (*Byzantine Style and Civilization*), and Vickers cited in the Bibliography.

25. Romano adduces Lucian, *The Ship* 26, presumably to illustrate the rare diminutive noun *psychidion*—the passage has no other relevance. Wilson does the same. But the word is not so rare as they think, being also present in the address to a dying soul quoted in the 3rd-century historian Dio Cassius 77. 16. 6a, an address strikingly similar to the famous apostrophe to his own soul in Latin by the Roman emperor Hadrian.

26. The author's verb (*suophagein*) may not be in any Greek lexicon, but the anti-Semitic tone is unfortunately not at all novel. For the sad story of the Jews in Byzantium, see Sharf, *Byzantine Jewry from Justinian to the Fourth Crusade.* Sharf, however, goes astray on the *Timarion*'s attitude, saying (144) that the Jews are significantly absent from the author's list (ch. 6) of visitors to the fair and that Jewish life in the area must have suffered in the wake of the Second Crusade because "it

is difficult to imagine that it (sc. *Timarion*) would have readily forgone a dig at the Jews." But as we know from the contemporary *Itinerary of Benjamin of Tudela* (ed. Adler), the Jews were already there as workers in the silk industry. It is they who attract the visiting textile merchants specified in the *Timarion*'s list. The author's allusion to pork constitutes his "dig." The context is appropriate: Benjamin of Tudela says that the Jews of Thessalonica were oppressed. The author's gibe is mild enough. One may suppose that he was not concerned to dig deeper, otherwise he might have made something out of the fact that Romanus IV Diogenes, kindly treated by him (20–22), had actually been blinded by a Jew: Michael Attaleiates, *Hist.* p. 178 Bonn.

27. Hunting was the sport of kings in Byzantine times. *Theodoros Prodromos, Historische Gedichte* (ed. Hörandner, p. 95), says the ideal emperor is the ideal hunter. Anna Comnena 3. 3 mentions that her royal father and brother hunted when free of state business.

28. Now the river Vardar, a name already current in the author's time, in fact used in their descriptions by Anna Comnena 1. 7 and Nicephorus Bryennius 4. 18 (p. 148 Bonn). As are most Byzantine writers, our author is inconsistent in such matters, veering as he does from this archaism to the vernacular "Bulgarian" in the very next sentence. Romano notes his indebtedness to Bryennius' description. I am also reminded of Herodotus' account of the Nile in Book Two of his history, an instinct confirmed by the presence of such Herodotean verb forms as *ekdidoi*. The Byzantines were addicted to elaborate pen portraits (the technical term for which is *ecphrasis*) of people, places, and things; there will be several more in the *Timarion*. Rivers were a favourite theme: Anna Comnena has at least six such purple passages; cf. Buckler 213 for references and discussion. In a letter to Michael Italicus (ed. Browning, *Byzantinobulgarica* 1 [1962], 279–97), Theodore Prodromos commends his *ecphrasis* of the Hebrus and other rivers. This is of interest, given my introductory canvassing of Italicus' claims to be the author of the *Timarion*. In addition

to displaying expertise in these literary conventions, Timarion shows himself to be an archetypal tourist, boastful of what he has seen. Thus, the Axios is the biggest river in Macedonia, the Hebrus (ch. 12) is the most famous river in Thrace, the fair at Thessalonica (ch. 5) is the biggest in Macedonia, and so on.

29. *Il*. 2. 653, and elsewhere.

30. Mention of old Macedonia and Pella would arouse suitable classical memories, in this case of Alexander the Great, in the author's readers, a constant aim of Byzantine literature.

31. In what follows, the author lets himself go linguistically, with one very rare phrase (*spermaton anadotikos*) along with a verb (*hoplitagogeo*) and an adjective (*athamnos*) said by Wilson to be absent from Greek lexica—the verb is actually in Stephanus. The military part of this *ecphrasis* reminds me, though not apparently Romano or Wilson, of Herodotus' description (6. 102) of the plain of Marathon, that place also being picked out for its suitability for cavalry. The fruitful and versatile soil in the first part anticipates, perhaps deliberately, the later (ch. 30) introduction of the garden oasis in Hades.

32. This picture of Phaedra calling to dogs and hunting is taken largely verbatim from Euripides, *Hippolytus* 218–9, lines long ago parodied by Aristophanes, fr. 51, preserved by Athenaeus 4. 133b. This passage should be of interest to students of the *Hippolytus*. For, as does Plutarch twice, it reproduces the two lines in the reverse order from that in Euripides' manuscripts, with the verb in the singular, forming a sequence that the best modern editor of the *Hippolytus,* W. S. Barrett (Oxford, 1964), says must be wrong because the verb *enchrimptesthai* can only be used of the hounds, not the hunter. If our author did not take his quotation from Plutarch rather than the original, he must have known a text of Euripides that differed from the extant ones. Either way, this is another example of how useful Byzantine literature can be to editors of classical texts.

33. For no obvious reason, the author here uses an unparalleled verb, the double compound *antepanelthomen,*

though despite Wilson it is recorded by Stephanus. Romano registers it as late Byzantine rather than unique, but gives no other example. There are at the most a dozen words in the *Timarion* not elsewhere attested. Not a high proportion for a text occupying 43 modern pages, certainly low compared to the contemporary satirist, Theodore Prodromos. In the index to his edition of Prodromos' historical poems, Hörandner lists around 250 unique formations, with a similar tally of very rare words. This statistic may tell against Hunger's notion (cf. the Introduction) that Prodromos could be the author of the *Timarion*. All linguistic data for Byzantine authors are, however, fragile to say the least, thanks to the crippling lack of indexes, often even of a reliable edition, and because of the complete inadequacy of the lexica of Ducange and Sophocles. A reliable lexicon is the most urgent need of Byzantinists.

34. The Greek is *kata ten deuteran tes kyrias; Deutera* is the modern Greek for Monday, *Kyriake* for Sunday.

35. Movie fans may here be reminded of the epigram of the French director Jean-Luc Godard to the effect that a film should have a beginning, a middle, and an end—but not necessarily in that order.

36. Homer, *Il.* 17. 1.

37. The Greek text here has *enon,* an accusative absolute doing service as the main verb. Wilson prefers Winterbottom's emendation *emon* ("it is not for me to . . ."), as does Macleod in his review of Romano, *JHS* 96 (1976), 271. Romano himself does not discuss the point, neither do Hase or Ellissen. But the Lucianic model for this section *Menippus or The Descent into Hell* 2, supports *enon.* For a similar, albeit not identical, extension of the accusative absolute, cf. Theodore Prodromos, *Ep.* 10 (*PG* 133. 1282B).

38. Comparison to a classical original is, of course, the ultimate Byzantine compliment. For the fair of Demetrius, see S. Vyronis in *The Byzantine Saint,* 202–4, where the *Timarion*'s account is discussed and extracts from it translated. Other saints in other cities were similarly honoured by what was partly a pagan tradition and by

what was to be adapted and perserved during the Ottoman occupation of Greece.

39. Not the original sense of Mysian, but used to denote the inhabitants of Moesia, the old Roman province between the Danube and the Balkan mountains, where a Slav-Bulgar kingdom had developed in the 7th century. In Tzetzes, *Ep.* 80 (ed. Leone 120. 19), someone is said to be "not Russian but Mysian"; cf. Shepard, *BF* 6 (1979), 191–240.

40. There are more egregious anachronisms in this register, for notable instance Iberians; they are here meant as Spaniards, but to the ordinary Byzantine the term now connoted Georgians. Portuguese and French also shelter behind the archaisms, as does the river Danube. No editor comments on the distinction drawn between Campanians (i.e. from Italy between Rome and Naples) and Italians; Greeks from southern Italy, where the Byzantine presence was finally liquidated in the Comnenan period, may be intended. It is nice to see that the author does not blame all these foreigners for corrupting the morals of Thessalonica, as does Cameniates, who indulges in xenophobia to find reasons for its sack in 904; cf. Kazhdan, *BZ* 71 (1978), 302. Of course, the author is himself a stranger from Cappadocia, either in reality or dramatically.

41. It is impossible to say whether this is a clue to the author's own background, or simply dramatic colouring. It has to be remembered that Cappadocians were proverbial bumpkins in classical humour, which would suit the narrator's role of awestruck tourist. For a sample Byzantine use of this ethnic as an insult, cf. the 10th-century Liutprand of Cremona, *The Embassy to Constantinople* 10.

42. A sensible thing to do, but the author may have been just as concerned to remind his audience of similar scenes in Lucian, *Charon* 5, and Heliodorus 5. 32. The biblical incident of Satan pointing out the wonders of the world to Christ during the latter's temptation could also have come to a Byzantine mind. Cameniates (p. 99 Bonn = *PG* 109. 585A) witnessed the sack of Thessalonica in 904 from a high vantage point.

43. Not "mechanisms" as in Vyronis' translation. For this meaning of the Greek *holkois,* Wilson adduces Nicander, *Theriaca* 266, but the author is more likely to have had in mind Lucian, *Hermotimus* 79.

44. A palpably Christian oath, as the Greek noun *Agape* makes clear.

45. Cf. Anna Comnena 15. 7 for an army "moving along like one huge beast."

46. For a good general account of the economy of the area, see Browning, *Byzantium and Bulgaria,* 102–15. More recent and detailed is Laiou-Thomadakis, *DOP* 34–35 (1980–1), 188. The commercial prosperity of late Byzantine Thessalonica is confirmed by Cydones, *Monody for the Dead of Thessalonica* (*PG* 109. 641). Such lists as the one that follows is very closely paralleled for Constantinople in the aforementioned (note 26) *Itinerary of Benjamin of Tudela.* What they contain is factual. Yet even here the author intends his audience to divine a classical pedigree, specifically Lucian, *The Syrian Goddess* 10.

47. This English version reproduces the effect of the Greek with its sequence (in grammatical asyndeton) of onomatopoeic verbs in the present participle (e.g. *grullizontes*). Notice the reason given for the presence of these animals. Anyone who has travelled by 4th-class rail in Greece will have seen the living paraphernalia often carted on the journey by peasants.

48. I have added the word "old-fashioned" to convey the classicising flavour of the Greek *architheoros.* The author seems to have got this and a few other words in the passage from Heliodorus' description (2. 35–3. 4) of a Delphic procession.

49. *Il.* 1. 477; *Od.* 2. 1. Although there is no reason to think that the author, who has it again in ch. 36, would not have got such a famous tag from the original, it remains noteworthy that it is also quoted in the above-mentioned section of Heliodorus; cf. also Lucian, *Imagines* 8; *Pro Imag.* 26. Dante twice (*Purg.* 2. 7–9; 9. 1.f.) personifies Dawn.

50. In deference to the usual demands of classicising style,

the author introduces the governor as *hegemon,* but by as early as the next chapter he has relapsed into the vernacular officialese of *doux* (from the Latin *dux*), albeit this is partly to signal his praise of the Ducas family. The presence of this official at the festival occasions no surprise: *noblesse oblige,* if nothing else, would have got him there. But it is still worth noticing a verse inscription in which a bishop and a governor are linked as founders of the basilica of St Demetrius: text and commentary in Halkin, *AB* 70 (1952), 129.

51. Vyronis oddly translates the Greek word for infantrymen (*pezon*) as "cavalry."

52. In adding this name to the translation I indicate agreement with Romano that the Greek *meteoros ho demos* is a conscious reflection of Thucydides 2. 8, though cf. Lucian, *Zeus Rants* 4; *Praise of Demosthenes* 28. This may help to explain the sudden grammatical shift in the Greek from singular to plural (*meteoros . . . karadokountes*), even though this is far from uncommon in Byzantine Greek and natural in the context of any collective noun.

53. A similar allusion to golden hair in the poems of Nicolas Callicles is exploited by Romano as one of his arguments for the former's authorship of the *Timarion.* But their common source is surely Homer, *Il.* 1. 197, especially as the author has just quoted *Il.* 13. 519; 17. 210–11, for the Ares comparison. Lucian, *Hermotimus* 9, might be a further influence on the *Timarion.* The Homeric tag was ubiquitous, being (for easy instance) on display in such an unpretentious text as *Life of St Triphyllios* 6, ed. Halkin, *AB* 66 (1948), 17. There are also the epithets *xanthokomes,* used by Pindar and Theocritus, and *xanthothrix* in Constantine Manasses, *Hodoiporikon* 1. 168; the latter (1. 172) also has the phrase *katachrysos kome.*

54. *Od.* 6. 230; 23. 157. In this sentence, my translation "concentrated on" takes the adverb *periergoteros* with what follows in the Greek ("contemplating his hair") rather than with the preceding "Homer's lines" as does Vyronis. Ellissen and Wilson understand it as I do, plac-

ing a comma after *poietou* in the text; Romano has no comma, but takes it the same way.

55. In these first two sentences the Greek is contorted and difficult, a common consequence when a Byzantine author embarks on this type of *ecphrasis*.

56. Vyronis translates "and let loose, like the air they turned away from the ground," which I do not follow.

57. Despite Wilson, the verb *hypoterpomenoi* is in Stephanus.

58. From the late Roman empire on, calmness of expression was *de rigueur* for an emperor in his ceremonial *adventus* or arrival, and non-imperial bigwigs will have imitated this. The classic account is Ammianus Marcellinus 16. 10. 9–11, on the entry into Rome of Constantius II in A.D. 357. The Greek epithet *galenos* used here is standard of emperors; cf. Baldwin, *B* 52 (1982), 17. Constantine Manasses, *Hodoiporikon* 2. 68, applies it to a Ducas.

59. These mythological figures are a standard feature of processions in Greek and Roman art and literature; cf. Baldwin, *AC* 23 (1980), 115–20. My translation "ran . . . under him" retains the manuscript reading *hypotrechon*. Ellissen and Wilson (the latter without comment) print Hase's emendation *epetrechon* ("ran about"), to which Romano inclines and on which Vyronis' translation is based. For a similar jingle, and similar textual variants, see the *Schede tou myos* 430. 8 (ed. Papademetriou), once thought to be by Theodore Prodromos but now possibly by Constantine Manasses, where a mouse *hama epetroche kai hama apetreche*. The 13th-century romance *Callimachus and Chrysorrhoe* 202 has *anatrechon paretrechon*. But the manuscript reading of the *Timarion* is surely right, the humorous point being that the creatures were small enough to scamper under the legs of people and horses.

60. As Wilson notes, the verb *polypragmoneo* is here used without the pejorative sense it bore in Attic; cf. Michael Italicus, *Ep.* 2. Such shifts of nuance are frequent in Byzantine Greek. What Wilson does not observe is that the author had earlier (ch. 6) used the cognate adjective in the original bad sense.

61. My version reflects the deliberate repetitions of the Greek (*prota . . . megale . . . proton*). The author's expression *ta prota pherein* marks another semantic shift. In Attic Greek, it denoted winning the first prize. The Byzantine meaning is to hold a high position, as frequently in Anna Comnena: 2. 6; 9. 8; 10. 2; 12. 2, 5; 13. 4; 14. 9. Examples are easy to multiply, from an epigram of Gregory Nazianzenus in the *Greek Anthology* 8. 111 to a speech by Nicephorus Gregoras, ed. Leone, *B* 51 (1981), 223. 3. Romano's parallels from Lucian are thus irrelevant.

62. Here again the Greek text has two expressions used neutrally that had been pejorative in classical idiom.

63. The author repeats this reference to "old" as part of his oblique punning allusion to the dux. This allusive style of reference is used on other occasions by the author (chs. 18, 22, 43), though he is not consistent. An irritation to the modern student, these allusions were obviously intended to be recognised by the original audience. Just why a common technique should operate in the cases of an illustrious general, an old glutton, a faithful imperial retainer, and a diminutive spouter of verses is not clear, especially since between the dux and the others there is the added distinction of alive and dead. Exactly who the dux was is unclear; for discussion and references to the secondary literature, see both Romano's note and Polemis, *The Doukai*, 74, 153. Ellisen pointed to Michael Palaeologus Ducas, a distinguished general of the period. According to Cinnamus 2. 13; 4. 7, he was exiled by John II (1118–43) for a reason Cinnamus himself did not know, recalled by the next emperor Manuel I (1143–80), was governor at Thessalonica (cf. Runciman, *History of the Crusades,* vol. 2, 260), and died whilst campaigning at Bari in south Italy in 1156. This identification would afford a clue to the date of the *Timarion,* which might then fall between the accession of Manuel and 1156; cf. the Introduction. The equation is misleadingly presented as a certainty by Tozer, *JHS* 2 (1881), 245, Wilson, and Lamma, *Comneni e Staufer,* 188, n. 1, who goes so far as to say that the *Timarion*

was dedicated to him, an assertion for which there is no evidence. Polemis seems to favour the equation but is candid on the problems, noting that Michael may have been a grandson rather than son of George Palaeologus and Anna Ducaena, on whom see below. A case can be made for Nicephorus Ducas Palaeologus or an otherwise unknown brother, or Andronicus Ducas, all sons of George and Anna. Romano likes Andronicus because he was mourned in poems 6–10 of Nicolas Callicles, his candidate for the authorship of the *Timarion*.

64. On the above reckonings, he is most likely to have been George Palaeologus (making the grandfather of the dux his father Nicephorus), a relative and confidant of Alexius I, and a distinguished general in the war with the Normans. He is frequently mentioned by Anna Comnena; cf. Polemis, *The Doukai*, 74.

65. *Od.* 2. 188; 7. 157; 24. 51.

66. Wilson calls the Greek verb *hypopsithurizetai* "a strangely inappropriate use of a rare verb," reaching this opinion on the basis of *LSJ*, whose authors cite only the novelist Achilles Tatius 1. 5. But the word is not all that rare; there are patristic examples in Lampe, and passages from the early Byzantine historians in Stephanus. The *Timarion* has it twice more, chs. 35, 37. Moreover, the onomatopoeic quality of the verb is here ideal for the notion of awestruck whispers wafting over the sea. Is there also a hint of raillery?

67. That is, the Romans. Nicephorus Bryennius, *Hist.* pref. p. 13 Bonn, confirms this conceit on the part of the Ducas family; cf. Polemis, *The Doukai,* 3–4. Constantine Manasses, *Hodoiporikon* 1. 185–6, connects the highborn Western girl intended as the second bride of Manuel I with the blood of Julius Caesar. Other families made similar claims, e.g. the Phocadae linked themselves with the old Roman clan of the Fabii: Atteleiates, *Hist.* p. 218 Bonn.

68. Andronicus Ducas (before 1045–77), the elder son of John Ducas, brother of the emperor Constantine X Ducas (1059–67). He served with Romanus IV Diogenes in the latter's fateful campaign of 1071 but played him false and

returned to Constantinople, where he joined the conspiracy against the emperor; cf. note 140. For the full details of his career, see Polemis, *The Doukai*, 55–57. Anna Ducaena, the wife of George Palaeologus, was the second of his three daughters by his wife Maria, a Bulgarian princess. Polemis 74–75 assembles what little information we have on her; she is known to be dead by 1136. Her elder sister Eirene became the wife and empress of Alexius I.

69. Wilson hesitantly suggests "guarantee" for the Greek verb *brabeuo*. The requisite sense is confirmed in Theodore Prodromos' poem *Mensium Adornatio* 10, ed. *PMGM* 18, also in Tzetzes, *Ep.* 46, ed. Leone 67. 2. For similar uses of the cognate nouns *brabeus* and *brabeion*, cf. Theodore Prodromos, *Ep.* 8 (*PG* 133. 1275A); Cameniates, *PG* 109. 540D.

70. Possibly quoted from Lucian, *Demonax* 67.

71. *Nicomachean Ethics* 1129b28, where a scholiast says it comes from the lost *Melanippe* of Euripides. This work of Aristotle is echoed at least twice more in the present description.

72. Another typical Byzantine *ecphrasis*, marked by contorted Greek not always easy to translate, and notable for its medley of reminiscences of classical literature and the Bible. The wine-like eyes and milk-white teeth, for instance, derive from the Septuagint version of Genesis 49. 12, also worth noting for the fact that it thus weakens the force of Romano's parallel with Nicolas Callicles as an argument for the latter's claims to the *Timarion*. Cf. Constantine Manasses, *Hodoiporikon* 1. 167: *hyper to gala kai kale kai leukotrichous; ibid.* 172 has *symmetros*, which the *Timarion* also has in this section. For a similar *ecphrasis*, see Anna Comnena 13. 10 on Bohemond, son of the Norman Robert Guiscard and a prime threat to Byzantium at the time.

73. According to Wilson, "this must be the sense, however strange it seems, since the phrase is borrowed from Gregory of Nyssa, *Epistle* 1. 13." But a glance at *LSJ* will confirm that, taken in their classical sense, the words could add up to mean "make a prayer with respect to his well-being."

74. *Od.* 4. 230, though the author could have taken it from Lucian, *Alexander* 5, a parallel unnoticed by Romano.
75. A phrase closely modelled on Euripides, *Bacchae* 236, and one that might be added to the note in Dodd's edition (2nd rev., Oxford, 1960) on the controversy over what part of the body is there referred to—yet another example of the unnoticed value of Byzantine texts for editors of classical ones.
76. Romano denotes the Greek verb *entraneo* as a late one, citing no other examples; Wilson does not comment. Yet the verb is absent from all modern lexica and according to Stephanus is unique to this passage.
77. This is how I understand *ton logon tranon,* a phrase Wilson calls obscure, suggesting it may mean "displaying clearly his intelligence." But it seems clear from the end of this chapter that Timarion heard the great man speak. Cf. the similar expressions *tranoumenen* and *hypertranousthai ten glossan* in Theodore Prodromos, *Ep.* 8 (*PG* 133. 1269A), also *logo diatranoun, Schede tou myos* 432. 9.
78. These criteria are not so much aesthetic as moral, since the Byzantines were as bedevilled as their Greek and Roman predecessors by theories of physiognomy. For these, and their baneful effect on historical and other writing, cf. Baldwin, *B* 51 (1981), 8–21.
79. Sappho is often cited and alluded to by Byzantine writers, fresh combing of whom could conceivably yield new fragments. For one such case, cf. Browning, *CR* 10 (1960), 192–3. See in general Garzya, *JOB* 20 (1971), 2, n. 6, taking the *Timarion*'s allusion to imply direct knowledge of Sappho. But, as Browning notes, prose paraphrases of Sappho are not uncommon in such contemporary texts as Gregory of Corinth's commentary on Hermogenes (ed. Walz, *Rhetores Graeci* 7), and our author could have been inspired by handbooks of rhetoric that go back to the famous ones of Menander Rhetor.
80. Aristotle, *Nic. Eth.* 1145a29; Plato, *Meno* 99d; also in the paroemiographers.
81. The Greek interjection is *babae,* another item found in the poems of Nicolas Callicles, and so taken by Romano

as a clue to authorship. But we hardly need a precise source for so simple a word; and if we did, Nicolas Callicles is not the only candidate. A contemporary parallel is furnished by a speech of (possibly) Theodore Prodromos, ed. Kurz, *BZ* 16 (1907), 115. 119. Prodromos himself has it more than once in his letters, e.g. *Ep.* 13 (*PG* 133. 1285B). Cf. also Constantine Manasses, *Hodoiporikon* 4. 164; *Schede tou myos* 430. 22. In an earlier age, the emperor Leo VI "The Wise" employs it in 1. 7 of his Anacreontic poem on hell, ed. Christ-Paranikas. But what may be more to the point than all these, the word, like all of the supposed parallels with Nicolas Callicles assembled by Romano, occurs at least once in Lucian.

82. The apparent note of uncertainty may be meant to remind us that Timarion is a visitor to the festival from Cappadocia, and so not sure of all the details.

83. This is how Wilson understands the Greek; Vyronis renders "then was maintained, exactly, the office of the festival," which is awkward, if not unclear.

84. This use of "wing" (*pterugion*) in the architectural sense is rare. Wilson offers no other instance; Romano has an early one from a text cited in Eusebius, *Church History* 2. 23. 12. There is actually a contemporary example in Nicolas Mesarites, *Description of the Church of the Holy Apostles* 3. 1, ed. Downey, *TAPhilS* 47. 6 (1957), 857–924.

85. Anna Comnena 15. 7 implies this to be a rarity, for when praising her father for giving the church in his orphanage such a mixed choir, she says that this was after the example of Solomon. However, Philo, *On the Contemplative Life,* p. 102 Paris, says that they were a traditional feature; cf. Christ-Paranakis, *Anthologia Graeca Carminum Christianorum* lviii.

86. "Painful and baneful" preserves the assonance of the Greek.

87. From this point, the plot turns on Timarion's illness and its diagnosis. It is based on the theory, as old as Hippocrates (cf. Jones Loeb ed., Vol. 1, xlvi–li), that the body contains 4 elements or humours: blood, phlegm,

and black and yellow bile. Readers of Chaucer will recognise it; cf. Allbutt, *Greek Medicine in Rome,* 132–3, 263–9. One of Romano's arguments for Nicolas Callicles as the author of the *Timarion* is that its medical knowledge must be that of a professional such as Callicles himself. This notion, perhaps implicit in the suggestion of Wilson, *Byzantine Books and Bookmen,* 12, that the satire was a *pièce d'occasion* for a limited audience, is explicit in the conclusion of Temkin, *DOP* 16 (1962), 115, that its audience would need a "remarkable medical knowledge" to enjoy it. Certainly, as Romano's own notes show, a good deal of the author's medical vocabulary is that of Hippocrates and Galen. But this does not make him a doctor. A smattering of medical knowledge was routinely included in the Byzantine higher education curriculum. In Psellus' poem on medicine, ed. *PMGM* 203–43, as well as in the iambic poems on the Sacred Art by, respectively, Archelaus, Hierotheus, and Theophrastus, ed. *PMGM* 328–58, there is the routine statement that a poem on medicine is for the general benefit of grammarians, philosophers, and rhetoricians. One should also bear in mind the tradition of do-it-yourself medical manuals, especially popular with landowners and others away from the urban centres. This tradition goes back at least to the late Roman period; e.g., Marcellus of Bordeaux, *On Remedies,* pref. 3. 2, promises cures that do not require a physician; cf. Brown, *The Cult of the Saints,* 116. Hence one did not have to be a professional to read medical texts. Nor did one have to burn the midnight oil over them. There were plenty of literary short cuts to a basic knowledge; in addition to the aforementioned poems of Psellus and others, there were such things as Psellus' *Lexicon of Medical Terms,* ed. Boissonade, *Anecdota Graeca* 1. 233–41, and the unpretentious survey of the anonymous *On the Nature of Man,* ed. *PMGM* 303–4. Thus, any educated Byzantine would know enough to appreciate a comic routine about fever and bile. That it was a regular feature of satire is beyond dispute. The *Mazaris* opens with its hero being sent down to Hades by a temporarily fatal fever. Theodore Prodromos frequently exploited illness and doctors for his satires, for instance in his *The Executioner or Doctor,* ed. Podestà, *Aevum* 21 (1947), 12–25; for the doctor as a butcher, cf. Pliny, *Natural History* 29. 13. Less funny is Prodromos' horrifying account, *Epp.* 4–6, *PG* 133. 1249 f., of his sufferings from what has been interpreted as the first documented case in European literature of smallpox by P. S. Codellas, *BHM* 20 (1946), 207–15. He is at least as graphic as Timarion about his fever and vomiting; we can well understand why he portrays his illness in terms of going to Hades and back, and why he blasts Byzantine doctors for their incompetence. Constantine Manasses, *Hodoiporikon* 2. 16 f., has a description almost as harrowing; he also (3. 71–74) thinks little of the skill of the (as he terms them) Asclepiadae. Apart from satire, on which see Baldwin, *BF* 8 (1982), 19–28, and travel literature, descriptions of illness were also a regular feature of Byzantine epistolography; cf. Mullett, *Byzantium and the Classical Tradition,* 90. It is in the light of all this literary tradition that the *Timarion* must be read. One or two details could imply that the author had a more than ordinary knowledge. For instance, Galen, *On the Natural Faculties* 2. 9, says that autumn was the usual season for excess of black bile, which makes it appropriate that Timarion should so suffer in late October. On the other hand, this could have been knowledge no more profound than our recognition that colds and influenza are most likely to afflict us in winter. The unkindest modern cut of all may be that some scholars think black bile to be a chimera teetering between hypothesis and fantasy; cf. Simon, *SAMN* 6 (1980), 3–4.

88. For contemporary theories on what to do for the tertian and quartan fevers, cf. Nicolas Mesarites (note 84 above) 42. 2–3. It is a weakness of Romano's commentary that he ignores all the contemporary material, one reason for my stressing it in these notes.

89. In the Third Beggar Poem (possibly by Theodore Prodromos), ed. Hesseling-Pernot, the abbott-cum-amateur doctor prescribes bread and onion both with olive oil

and mint for a feverish monk. An anonymous *Mensium Adornatio,* ed. *PMGM* 422, enjoins caution in the use of vegetables in the case of *yellow* bile as they bring on a green one.

90. Mazaris (114) likewise improves briefly before his "death."

91. Nowadays, this might be dismissed as nothing more than a case of "Greek tummy."

92. The following description makes it clear that the competition amongst modern tourists to prove who had the worst experiences on their trip has a long pedigree. Cf. the earlier tribulations (note 87) of Constantine Manasses on his pilgrimage. For Timarion's furnace-like fever, Romano adduces Lucian, *On Salaried Men in Great Houses* 26, remarkably overlooking the latter's *Lover of Lies* 25, the model for this and other details, not only linguistic but also of content, including the central motif of death before one's time. These parallels will be pointed out in subsequent notes. One would not have thought Timarion's condition improved by his horse ride, but according to Eftychiadis, *SAMN* 9 (1982), 20, riding was one of the many prescriptions of early Byzantine physicians for fever.

93. As well as the reminiscence of Euripides detected in the Greek *ou biosimon* by Romano, there could be an echo of Herodotus 1. 45; 3. 109. But cf. *me biosima* in ch. 13, taken as Romano shows from Hippocrates and Galen.

94. Sleep as the relative of death is a notion as old as Homer, as Romano makes clear, but in a Byzantine context one should also observe that it is a common conceit in the Church Fathers. Notice also that the pagan Hades is frequently used in Christian epitaphs; cf. Lattimore, *Themes in Greek and Latin Epitaphs,* for many examples.

95. A conventional period in such situations. Mazaris suffered for 3 weeks (20 days plus 1 is how the Greek puts it); in Lucian, *Lover of Lies* 26, a man is resurrected 20 days after burial.

96. This combination of Christian angels and the pagan Hermes in his psychopompic role as conductor of the

dead to Hades is a cultural fusion typical of the *Timarion*, an element that excited the wrath of Constantine Acropolites. The author gets his avenging angels, both fact and phrase, from Plutarch, *Roman Questions* 51, where they are associated with the Greek Stoic thinker Chrysippus. On these pagan-Christian Interrelationships, see Gokey, *The Terminology for the Devil and Evil Spirits in the Apostolic Fathers*. Timarion's abduction to Hades and reception there is a sustained parody of common, if unofficial, Byzantine belief. Demons would rush to the deathbed of an expiring human to battle for possession of his soul with a guardian angel. The soul flew through the air and attempted to get by a variety of customs posts, where officiating demons would check its earthly record and either let it through or exact payment. This infernal bureaucracy was very efficient, having complete records on all comers; cf. *Timarion* 15, where the guards know at once who the narrator is. There is some obvious affinity in all of this with classical beliefs of the sort regularly parodied by Lucian. But as Mango, *Byzantium: The Empire of New Rome,* 164—an account on which I have drawn—points out, this rigmarole is a graphic representation of the burden of bureaucracy on earth and the Byzantine fear of the tax collector.

97. Neither Romano nor Tozer in the extract translated in *JHS* 2 (1881), 246, make anything of the Greek particle *ede* ("already"). But it may be a nice artistic touch, emphasising the narrator's anger at his premature taking.

98. The author is not consistent in his classical details, since Pluto never appears. He also ignores Rhadamanthus, the other traditional judge of the underworld, who does feature in the *Mazaris* (115). In Dante, between whom and the *Timarion* there are several interesting points of difference and similarity (each to be noted as it crops up), Minos judges alone (*Inf.* 5. 45) and Pluto is confused with the god of wealth Plutus (*Inf.* 6. 115 f.).

99. Sleep, an obvious expedient in times of sickness, is recommended for attacks of the yellow bile by the aforementioned (note 89) *Mensium Adornatio*. More to the

point is Lucian, *Lover of Lies* 25, where the narrator is also lying awake at the moment of his visitation. Lucian's victim, however, sees not two dirty black devils but a handsome white-cloaked youth who will be recalled by the *Timarion*'s description in ch. 33 of the angel of the emperor Theophilus.

100. The Greek here is similar to Lucian, *The Dream* 5, and may be the source; Romano does not notice the parallel. As a student of philosophy, Timarion needs a good excuse for losing his powers of judgement. The breakdown of philosophical theory in the face of reality is a common element in classical satire.

101. The classical god of healing, later treated roughly in the satire.

102. Or, to convey the flavour of the Greek *homonekros,* "show some esprit de corpse." Romano denotes *homonekros* as a late Greek word, giving no other example. In Stephanus and *LSJ* the only reference is to Lucian, *Dialogues of the Dead* 2. 1, presumably our author's inspiration.

103. Apparently the meaning of the Greek *aperiskeles,* only found here according to Stephanus and not in *LSJ* or other modern lexica.

104. The Greek adjective *ouriodromos* is not indicated by Romano as in any way rare, but Stephanus gives only this passage and it is absent from LSJ and other lexica. I have come across one other example, in a poem written by Alexius I to his son John, 1. 253, ed. Maas, *BZ* 22 (1913), 348–62, who thought it unique there. It could be the reading in Constantine Manasses, *Hodoiporikon* 2. 8, where Horna has *ouriodromoun* from the cognate verb.

105. A traditional feature of the classical approach to the underworld. An educated man such as the narrator would have known this, so what is the point of the following qualification about this being what his guides called it? The point is perhaps that the old names have not been replaced by Christianity, hence the classicising paraphernalia are justified, something that would anticipate if not deflect the criticism of Constantine Acropolites. Com-

pare the ambivalent attitude of Dante, *Parad.* 8. 1. f., towards the quality and error of pagan myths; cf. J. Sinclair's note in his editions. As to the unnamed river, my version agrees with Tozer's understanding of the ambiguous Greek *potamon hon ho logos onomase prolabon* as alluding to the Styx, over which the narrator and guides have to fly, since Charon does not feature in the *Timarion*'s vision of Hades. Romano, who has no note, translates "che il discorso precedentemente nomino," which seems to take it as referring to one of the earthly rivers already mentioned in Timarion's narrative.

106. To Romano's classical and patristic parallels, we may add Lucian, *Lover of Lies* 25, also the description of hell in the aforementioned poem of Leo VI (cf. note 18).

107. Romano here detects an echo of Julian, *Oration* 7. 210a, which would be an interesting reflection of late Byzantine acquaintance with the work of that apostate emperor (cf. note 126). A precise source may be thought unnecessary for so simple a Greek phrase. However, although unremarked by Romano, there does seem to be a more palpable echo of the same passage in the next chapter, where mountain bandits are alluded to; if so, this would strengthen the claims of the present parallel.

108. The iron gate of Hades is a traditional detail, as early as Homer, *Il.* 8. 15, and significantly in at least two of the spurious dialogues ascribed to Lucian: *Affairs of the Heart* 32; *The Patriot* 23.

109. Compare Dante, *Inf.* 1. 31–36, 46, 49, where his descent is variously blocked by a leopard, a lion, and a she-wolf. Dragons guard the ogre's castle in *Callimachus and Chrysorrhoe* 188 f. For the cognate situation of dragons watching over an underground treasure, see Saint Basil's essay, *On Greek Education* 9. 92–94, ed. Wilson (London, 1975), who adduces the Roman fabulist Phaedrus 4. 21, adding "I do not know a Greek text of it."

110. The famous three-headed dog, although from what follows it is clear that he is now much tamed, in contrast to Dante, *Inf.* 6. 13. f., where the traditional sops are required. It is notable that the infernal ferryman Charon does not appear in the *Timarion*, although Lucian made

good satiric use of him, as do other Byzantine satires, the *Mazaris* (117–8) for instance, also Theodore Prodromos' aforementioned (note 87) attack on doctors, 20. 16–17. Charon is also on duty in Dante, *Inf.* 3. 82. f.

111. From here to the end of this chapter is largely recycled from 13–14. The same clumsy repetition will be seen on a larger scale in ch. 25, where the narrator tells his old master what he has already told at length to Kydion. Like many a modern playwright, the author has not mastered the problem of how to dispense necessary information to audience and characters without tedious iteration.

112. Kydion at last makes a sensible observation, albeit he owes it to Lucian, *On Grief* 2.

113. Torches are used in Lucian, *Menippus or The Descent into Hell* 9. But the detail is worth emphasising *à propos* the realities of ancient technology and Byzantine life. Few actions of the controversial 5th-century prefect Cyrus of Panopolis were more popular than his provision of evening and night lights outside workmen's shops; cf. Baldwin, *B* (1980), 45.

114. Thus Romano also, though Tozer, *JHS* 2 (1881), 249, takes the Greek adjective *agoraios* as referring to the middle classes, albeit in the next chapter it must refer to a commoner.

115. It is pleasant to record that this will be Kydion's last intrusion until the penultimate chapter.

116. The Greek verb *synupantao* is not in any lexicon and might be the author's coinage; cf. note 33.

117. A nice (and rare) glimpse into a Byzantine schoolroom. For a fascinating new text about schooling in late antiquity, cf. Dionisotti, *JRS* 72 (1982), 83–125. On the early Byzantine centuries, see Moffatt, *Iconoclasm*, 85–92. A depressing look at schooling in the author's own time, full of grammatical lists to learn, and much talk of physical punishments, is provided by the grammatical poem of Nicetas of Heraclea, ed. Boissonade, *Anecdota Graeca* 2. 340–93, on which see Tovar, *Classical Studies Presented to B. E. Perry*, 223–35.

118. This may not sound appetising to us, but it is typical

Byzantine fare, especially the fatty meat; the author of the Beggar Poems (cf. note 89) is always dreaming of such meals. For the disgusted reaction of the Western palate of Bishop Liutprand of Cremona, a diplomatic visitor to Constantinople in the 10th century, see the remarks of Weber in *Liutprand von Cremona in Konstantinopel.*

119. He must certainly have lost his sense of taste, since (in satirical literature, at least) it is unheard of for a Byzantine to decline a free meal. But (not for the first time) the author is inconsistent: two dead men will appear, chs. 21, 26, who both retain their keen interest in earthly foods.

120. As did the Palaeologan family described earlier, which makes it likely that, as Ellissen, Tozer, and Romano think, this anonymous glutton is a relative or close acquaintance of the dux at Thessalonica. It is usual to say in such oblique matters that the author provides his original audience with enough clues to recognise the character but refrains out of caution from naming him. That technique might get him round modern laws of libel, but is not altogether logical since if the reader could recognise the victim, why could not the victim himself or his friends? Perhaps because such characters were a common object of literary satire, e.g. Theodore Prodromos, *Against a Long-bearded Old Man*, ed. Boissonade, *Anecdota Graeca* 4. 430–5.

121. The Greek in this sentence is full of wordplays on death and shelter and on richness of years and fat.

122. Keeping a pig at home to fatten and kill for food is still quite common amongst poor people (my own family in Britain did it in the 1950s). For an extreme case, see the 12th-century critic Tzetzes, *Ep.* 18 (ed. Leone 34–37), describing the horrors of living beneath an apartment full of children and pigs that produced so much urine that ships could have floated on it. British readers may here think of John Arden's play *Live Like Pigs*.

123. See *Mazaris* 126 for this thought. A variant, to the effect that things on earth may be worse than in Hades, is expressed in a letter of Psellus published by Snipes, *GRBS* 22 (1981), 89–107.

124. Theodore Prodromos wrote one comic piece about mice, a parody of Euripidean drama entitled *Battle of the Mice* (*Katomyomachia,* ed. Hunger), also perhaps the aforementioned *Schede tou myos.* The modern reader will think of Winston Smith's abomination of rats in Orwell's *1984.*

125. Hatred of mice is a common theme in Hellenistic and Byzantine epigram, e.g. *Greek Anthology* 6. 302, 303; Christopher of Mitylene (11th century), Poem 103. On their greed, cf. Pliny, *NH* 10. 85. 185; Aelian, *Nature of Animals* 5. 14; 17. 7. Apart from the narrator's own phobia, mice were a nuisance in that they often ate or nibbled at books, a common motif in classical satire: Anon. in Quintilian 8. 3. 19; Juvenal 3. 207; *Philogelos* 8 (a jokebook compiled in the 5th or 6th century, ed. Thierfelder, Munich, 1968). A real-life case is reported in *Pap. Zenon* 2033. In the well-known relief of Homer by Archelaus, two mice are depicted nibbling a roll; cf. West, *HSCP* 73 (1969), 123, n. 35. I remember once reading in the *Times* that mice ate bank notes worth 3 million pounds in the bank vaults of the Nizam of Hyderabad. For the theme of mice nibbling away at the possessions of the rich and great, see Lucian, *The Cock* 24; *Zeus Rants* 8.

126. The author may here be influenced by Julian, *Beard Hater* 338c, where lice rather than mice live in a beard and profit from the sloppy greed of the man. We know from Theodore Prodromos, *Ep.* 5, that Julian's satire was read at this time. Anna Comnena 15. 6 describes the dream of Malik-Shah (a Turkish emir of the period) in which many mice surrounded him at breakfast trying to snatch away the food and then turned into lions and overcame him.

127. My translation of the verb *ektragodei,* which Romano takes to refer only to the sound of the snores, but which in this context of a sleeping glutton might allude to the *Cyclops* of Euripides, his satyr play based on the Homeric monster; cf. note 133.

128. Roughly half a mile.

129. The Greek *skene* is ambiguous, since it means both tent

(which is how Tozer here takes it) or dwelling place in general, as for example in Mesarites 3. 1, ed. Downey; cf. Stilwell (ed.), *Antioch on the Orontes,* vol. 2, p. 46, n. 10. According to the index by Gautier to the Budé edition of Anna Comnena, *skene* only means tent in her history. Romano translates "tabernacolo," which according to the *Cambridge Italian Dictionary* is obsolete for tent or pavilion, and which in modern idiom means shrine or tabernacle. To have Romanus in a tent in Hades would be a good ironic touch on the author's part, since the unfortunate emperor had been invited to a feast in Andronicus' tent prior to his arrest and blinding: Psellus, *Chron.* 7. 41. The historian Attaleiates, p. 113 Bonn, has him in a tent just before battle, sketching out his plan of campaign.

130. Timarion will presently (ch. 22) be informed by a denizen of the underworld that this pitiable figure is the former emperor Romanus IV Diogenes. Blinding was an all too frequent Byzantine punishment of deposed emperors, failed usurpers, and suspect princes or generals. Along with similar barbarities, it was first prescribed as a regular penalty in the *Ecloga* or Law Code of the iconoclast emperor Leo III in 726. The sources agree that Romanus was blinded with particular ferocity; the chronicler Scylitzes, p. 705 Bonn (*PG* 122. 435A) describes his eyes as "dug out" (*exororugmenous*).

131. Romano evinces surprise that the rug is Spartan rather than Persian or Armenian, but the author has already (ch. 6) mentioned the Peloponnese in association with textiles; anyway, the classical connotations of Spartan austerity would suit the image of the warrior emperor Romanus.

132. A very similar description is given by Scylitzes, p. 664 Bonn (*PG* 122. 393A), who adds the detail that Romanus had handsome eyes, a grim irony in the context of his blinding and one that the satirist notably excludes.

133. *Il.* 16. 776; cf. *Od.* 24. 40. The tag was a common one, on show in such unpretentious texts as the scraps of verse honouring the ascetic St Sisoes, ed. Halkin, *AB* 66 (1948), 89. Similarly, Psellus, *Chron.* 7. 3, cites *Il.* 15.

678 to describe the size of Romanus' armour. The satirist's ensuing comparison with a wooded peak is from *Od.* 9. 190–1, though it may be doubted if the author was fully alive to its suitability here. For Homer is describing the Cyclops, to which gross, one-eyed monster Romanus could only be compared in tasteless mockery. In the original, Homer was emphasising the creature's lonely life, hence the mountain peak image; "grain-eating" is masterly irony, since the Cyclops is presently revealed to be a cannibal. But see my earlier suggestion (note 127) that the author may have been reading the *Cyclops* of Euripides.

134. Again, Timarion will be presently informed as to his identity.

135. There is nothing about poison in the accounts of Romanus' death by Psellus, Bryennius (pp. 54–55 Bonn = *PG* 127. 90B–D), Anna Comnena, or for that matter such distinguished modern historians as Ostrogorsky, *History of the Byzantine State,* 345. Anna, incidentally, was inclined (15. 6) to blame Romanus for the problems of the empire, albeit not to the degree alleged by Buckler 261. Psellus, of course, is particularly untrustworthy on the subject of Romanus because of the need to whitewash his pupil, the next emperor Michael VII. The contrast between his version in the *Chronography* and the eulogy in his letter to Constantine, nephew of the patriarch Cerularius, written whilst accompanying Romanus on campaign (cf. note 123), is blatant. The poisoning is mentioned in the chroniclers Scylitzes, p. 705 Bonn (*PG* 122. 435A), who is concerned to disparage Psellus, and Zonaras 18, p. 285 Bonn (*PG* 135. 275B), also by Attaleiates, pp. 175–6 Bonn. These discrepancies reflect the politics and personalities of the times, and the satirist's choice of version is one indication of his feelings, not only towards Romanus but also those who came after him. See later (chs. 41 f.) for Timarion's ambivalent reactions to Psellus himself. In the present context, notice finally the occasional linguistic similarity between this passage and Psellus' account of the poisoning of the earlier emperor Romanus III, *Chron.* 3. 26.

136. The Greek adjective *marasmodes* is cited in Stephanus and *LSJ* only from medical writers; its presence here may be indicative either of the author's scientific knowledge or his capacity for reproducing it from books.

137. Romano denotes the Greek *neonekros* as a late word, giving no parallel; Stephanus cites only this passage, and *LSJ* does not have it. The epithet might be a coinage of the author to go with the introduction of the old-timer (*palaios*).

138. As earlier observed, gluttony is a cardinal theme of classical and Byzantine satire. The narrator's old teacher, soon to appear, is similarly obsessed with food. With the exception of Homer's heroes, who mainly eat meat, fish of all sorts were a common delicacy in Greece—the comedies of Aristophanes abound with jokes about them. Thus, as often, the satirist is combining literary allusion with Byzantine reality. It might be added that Timarion's Hades does not have the advantage of the waters of Lethe, as in the *Mazaris*, where (126) they can be withheld as a punishment.

139. Romano has no comment on the adjective *mychiaios,* although it gains only an unreferenced mention in Stephanus and is not in *LSJ* or other modern lexica.

140. Romanus IV Diogenes reigned 1068–71, succeeding Constantine X Ducas, whose widow Eudocia he married, a match opposed by the late emperor's brother, the caesar John, and by Psellus. On the etymology of his name Diogenes ("Zeus-born," thereby giving him the aura of an Homeric hero), see Attaleiates, p. 100 Bonn. According to the sympathetic Norman historian William of Apulia, *The Deeds of Robert Guiscard,* ed. *MGHAA* 9 (Berlin, 1851), 239–98, the name derived from his large beard (*barba bifurris);* cf. Mathieu, *B* 20 (1950), 90. William, incidentally, does not mention the poison attempt on Romanus. In spite of the depreciation by Psellus and Anna, Romanus was a good and experienced general, just what the empire needed at the time. His campaign against the Seljuk Turks, which had to be undertaken with a largely mercenary army, began well with successes in 1068 and 1069, but then came to grief

in the battle of Mantzikert near Lake Van in Armenia on August 19, 1071. The rest of Romanus' story is as the satirist summarises it, though like Psellus he avoids the fact that the emperor's defeat was largely caused by the treachery of Andronicus Ducas, son of the caesar John. Romanus is the only Byzantine emperor in the *Timarion,* apart from Theophilus, whom we encounter later. Quite why he should attract this detailed attention is uncertain. He was not the news of the moment in Constantinople, since the satire was written quite a few years later. The simplest solution is to say that the author wanted to give prominence to a fellow Cappadocian, a notion that assumes that the narrator's origins are more than a dramatic colouring. A desire to counter the version of Psellus might be a factor. And the author may simply have recognised that the battle of Mantzikert was a turning point in Byzantine history, as do modern writers; cf. Friendly, *The Dreadful Day.*

141. The Greek text reads *paraspondethon,* emended to *-etheis* by Hase and by Ellissen) and *-edon* by Garzya, which Romano prints. Whatever suffix be preferred, we are left with an otherwise unattested word. But Theodore Prodromos has *paraspondetes* in one of his historical poems, 4. 163 ed. Hörandner, who notes it as a rarity.

142. Another Great Phrygian. This one was first plausibly identified with Cututarius (or Chatatoures), duke of Antioch, by Dräseke, *BZ* 6 (1897), 485, on the basis of Bryennius 1. 21, p. 47 Bonn. On his career, cf. Laurent, *BZ* 30 (1929–30), 405–11, who does not notice the *Timarion* allusion. Dräseke did not observe that the Bryennian account is also in Psellus, *Chron.* 7. 34, though Cututarius is not there named and with the significant addition, "a crafty fellow, opposed to us on principle." According to the verse chronicle of Constantine Manasses (*PG* 127. 466A), Romanus was "friendless and deserted."

143. For this metaphorical use of the late and infrequent verb *dionko,* cf. Eunapius, *Lives of the Sophists* 478; Romano marks it as late, offering no parallel.

144. The description and circumstances of this encounter are strikingly similar to Dante's meeting with the now scorched-looking Brunetto Latini, *Inf.* 15. 22 f. I gather from Dante scholars that the ambivalent attitude shown by the poet to Latini is a great puzzle. Although dramatically natural, indeed necessary, the meetings and conversation Timarion has in Hades have a long literary pedigree, from Homer, *Od.* 11, to the dialogues of Lucian, to such contemporary exercises as Nicephorus Basilaces, *What Ajax Might Say on Seeing Odysseus in Hades with His Body,* ed. Walz, *Rhetores Graeci* 1. 473–5. Mango, *Byzantium: The Empire of New Rome,* 147, is a little cruel in observing that encountering this stuff in Byzantium makes one feel the clock had been stopped for a thousand years. These exercises were similar to the little essays of historical and literary imagination my generation did at school; looking back, they were very good mental training.

145. If we must look for a source for the Greek, Herodotus 1. 8; 3. 38; 7. 18 (*ambosas mega*) is as likely as Euripides, *Bacchae* 1079, adduced by Romano.

146. Having earlier (ch. 5) employed a distinctive Christian oath, the author now puts in one that looks just as pagan. The discrepancy may in fact disclose some subtlety of characterisation. A Christian oath suits the narrator who subsequently (ch. 27) makes a parade—sincere or otherwise—of his piety, whereas a pagan idiom would spring naturally from the lips of a professional Byzantine sophist.

147. As we shall see, Timarion's teacher was a notable glutton, hence good dinners are bound to bulk large in his memory. The implied social intimacy between professor and student is worth modern attention, if not envy. For similar Roman situations, see Aulus Gellius, *Attic Nights* 7. 13; 17. 8; and elsewhere. This academic sense of "chair" gives us the modern usage. The grander title going with it was consul of the philosophers, a pomposity not hard to parallel in modern European acadamese. It was held successively by Psellus, John Italus, and Theodore of Smyrna, all of whom feature in the *Timar-*

ion's underworld. The precise history and impact of the university in Constantinople is obscure and disputed, as are many details of Byzantine organisation of tertiary education. Originally founded in A.D. 425 by Theodosius II, it has vanished from sight by the early 7th century, then is apparently revived in 1045. The classic modern account is Fuchs, *Die höheren Schulen von Konstantinopel im Mittelalter.* Anglophone readers of the *Timarion* might profit most from Hussey, *Church and Learning in the Byzantine Empire 867–1185,* especially for its full discussions of Psellus and John Italus. For some recent and characteristically polemical remarks, cf. Mango, *Byzantium: The Empire of New Rome,* 129–31.

148. A very Byzantine quandary.
149. As stated above, Theodore of Smyrna (a city long famous for producing rhetoricians) succeeded Psellus and John Italus to the office of consul of the philosophers. He seems to have played a role in the Synod of Blachernae which closed in 1094. Along with Theodore Prodromos and others, he joined in the dispute with the Latin Church c. 1112 over the nature of the Holy Ghost; cf. Runciman, *The Eastern Schism,* 108–9. He wrote commentaries on the physical theories of Aristotle which are not yet published. In general, along with references to the specialised periodical literature, see Hussey, *Church and Learning in the Byzantine Empire 867–1185, 104, 111–2;* Beck, *Kirche und theologische Literatur im byzantinischen Reich,* 616–7; Browning, *Balkan Studies* 2 (1961), 181; Romano 138. Cf. the introduction for more on his chronology and its relationship to the date of the *Timarion.*
150. This translation attempts to preserve the punning Greek adjective *lamyros,* meaning both "fat" and "famous," a play on words repeated in ch. 39.
151. This Greek here is *eumegetheia,* a noun nowhere else attested, perhaps coined out of need to vary the descriptions of Theodore's size.
152. Romano adduces Poem 24 of Nicolas Callicles for the topic of arthritis, no doubt in pursuit of his authorship theory. But it need not, indeed cannot, be so restricted.

Similar situations are easy to come by in Byzantine life and literature. Psellus, *Chron.*, 2. 7, describes Constantine VIII as so crippled by gluttony that he could not walk. There is similarity of language and situation in *Mazaris* 142. Nor does Romano notice Lucian, *The Cock* 10, where the philosopher Thesmopolis is thus afflicted.

153. Usually in Byzantine satire, men of letters complain about their poverty and lack of recognition; Tzetzes and Prodromos are good examples. The fourth Beggar Poem perhaps best sums up the aspirations and disappointments of literary men of this period; cf. Trypanis, *Penguin Book of Greek Verse*, 442–3, for a translation, also Kyriakis, *B* 44 (1974), 290–309. Rates of payment would naturally vary according to an emperor's tastes and budget. In earlier times, e.g. Oppian in the 3rd century and John Lydus in the 6th, writers sometimes enjoyed the enviable reward of one gold coin per line of verse, something designed to produce long poems.

154. Stephanus found no other example of the Greek *lithoma,* and it is absent from modern lexica.

155. The life-style is indeed Epicurean—in the classical sense—though the author probably derives it from Lucian, who often, e.g. *The Cock* 23, recommends this prescription for true happiness.

156. Contrast (it is unnoticed by Romano) Lucian, *The Downward Journey* 2, where there are complaints over asphodel as food.

157. *Works and Days* 40–41, a tag amusingly enough to be found also in *Ep.* 178, ed. Delehaye, *AB* 51 (1933), 278, of the *Timarion*'s detractor, Constantine Acropolites.

158. The Greek *demoprepes* is not in any modern lexicon; Stephanus found no other example. Ellissen printed (without discussion) his own conjecture *demoterpes* ("crowd-delighting"), which is palaeographically attractive but probably not necessary. Romano ignores the matter.

159. I do not see why Romano thinks this final clause is taken from Homer, *Od.* 11. 171, since the thought is unexceptional and the only word the two passages have in common is *thanatos* ("death").

160. In fact, we get a tedious recapitulation of chs. 11–15. This discouraging habit of following up a promise of brevity with the opposite was by no means uniquely Byzantine. Readers of Cicero, for easy instance, soon find out that his formula *quid maius?* ("why say more?") is an inevitable prelude to prolixity.

161. The Greek is *aori ton nykton*. Romano translates *aori* separately, but the entire phrase can by itself mean just "dead of night" in Lucian and elsewhere. Mazaris (115, 124) was similarly snatched away *aori nykton*.

162. A mode of spiritual egress derived from the apocryphal *Apocalypse of Esdras* 56.

163. Homer, *Il.* 16. 856, 22. 362, also quoted in Theodore Prodromos' satire *Plato-Lover*, ed. Podestà, *Aevum* 21 (1947), 10. 8–9.

164. Timarion's cynicism about earthly courts and justice is paralleled in detail by *Mazaris* 126–7. Such grievances had long been standard and were by no means restricted to satire. In the famous account (fr. 8) by the 5th-century historian Priscus of his visit to the camp of Attila the Hun, a renegade Greek is encountered who largely blames the corruption of justice for his decision to go and live with the barbarians. Cf. Morris, *PP* 73 (1976), 3–27.

165. So much for Theodore's diet of asphodel.

166. As was earlier seen (note 98), no mention is made of Rhadamanthus, who does however feature in *Mazaris* 115.

167. This detail is presumably one that did much to excite the wrath of Constantine Acropolites. Gregory Nazianzenus, *Oration* 4. 76 (*PG* 35. 601B) denounces Julian for always calling the Christians "Galilaeans." As indeed the emperor did, using the label in the title of his treatise *Against the Christians* and elsewhere (e.g. *Ep.* 89). His motive is obvious: reduce the enemy from world religion to unimportant local cult. The only other use of the term given in Lampe is that by Manes to insult the orthodox. In the balance of the sentence, Romano sees in the word *mystes* ("disciple" or "initiate") an echo of Euripides, *Cretans* (fr. 472. 10, ed. Nauck). This is pos-

sible, in view of Minos the Cretan in the next chapter, but not necessary, since a glance at Lampe shows that *mystes* is commonly applied to followers of Christ.

168. The classical importance of Aesculapius or Asclepius and his relationship with the medical profession is best studied in Behr, *Aelius Aristides and the Sacred Tales*. Hippocrates, Galen, and Aesculapius are figures of ridicule in the disputes between doctors and healing saints in the hagiographical tradition; cf. Magoulias, *BZ* 57 (1964), 127–50. He is one of the gods most roughly handled in the Apology of the 2nd-century Church Father Aristides, a diatribe reproduced in the Christian romance *Barlaam and Ioasaph* traditionally ascribed to St John Damascene, and most recently in excerpts in 2 manuscripts of the 15/16th centuries published by Sinkewicz, *Byz. St.* 9. 2 (1982), 211–9, who unaccountably mistakes the *Barlaam and Ioasaph* for Barlaam of Calbria. Since Aesculapius had in the traditional mythology been blasted by a thunderbolt from Zeus for presuming to raise the dead, we can well understand his present condition.

169. That is to say, Greeks whose dialect was Attic rather than Ionic, the dialect employed by Hippocrates (also the historian Herodotus), a brogue parodied more than once by Lucian, in whose time it enjoyed an attempted renaissance, hence the author's exploitation of it here.

170. The author's ridicule of this Hellenistic doctor (c. 300 B.C.) is no doubt influenced by Galen's professional depreciation of him. Modern scholars are very favourable to his scientific work; cf. Allbutt, *Greek Medicine in Rome*, 149–56; Phillips, *Greek Medicine*, 45–55. Of particular relevance to the *Timarion* is Erasistratus' minimising of the humoral theory—he never mentions black bile.

171. The Greek diminutive *doxarion* is quite rare; the author probably got it from Lucian, *Peregrinus* 8, not noticed by Romano.

172. Antiochus, eldest son of king Seleucus of Syria, fell in love with his own stepmother Stratonice—a reversal of the situation in the *Hippolytus* of Euripides. Diagnosing

his malady, Erasistratus, the highly paid royal doctor, tricked Seleucus into a promise whereby he was obliged to divorce Stratonice and allow his son to marry her. The story is told by Plutarch, *Demetrius* 38, and Appian, *Syrian Wars* 11. 10. Its presence in the *Patria Cpoleos,* ed. Preger 2. 157. 14, shows that it was well known in Byzantine times.

173. Along with Hippocrates, Galen was one of the two most celebrated and influential of ancient doctors. In his career, which spanned most of the 2nd century A.D., he achieved the position of physician to Marcus Aurelius. There is a good account of his life and works in Sarton, *Galen of Pergamum.* His voluminous writings (they fill 20 volumes in the standard modern edition of Kuhn), surviving in both Greek and Arabic, show him to have been deeply interested in the literary and philosophical issues of his day, as is also evidenced by his friendship with Lucian and his appearance in the *Learned Men at Dinner* of Athenaeus. A major factor in his continuing fame was the large role his work played in Christian theology, not so much for its medical as its philosophical content; cf. Walzer, *Galen on Jews and Christians,* 77, based on Eusebius, *Church History,* 5. 28. This may be why Dante, *Inf.* 4. 130 f., places him in the circle of philosophers headed by Aristotle. As Meyer (quoted by Allbutt, *Greek Medicine in Rome,* 299) said, he was "for Rome an episode, for the Middle Ages an epoch." For the widespread Byzantine, Latin, and Arabic knowledge of and work on him around the *Timarion*'s time, see Temkin, *Galenism: Rise and Decline of a Medical Philosophy,* 95–133; cf. Greppin, *SAMN* 9 (1982), 111–3, for Armenian interest. According to Oestreich, *Classical Influences on European Literature A.D. 1500–1700,* ed. Bolgar, 316, there were 660 editions of Galen in the period 1490–1598. One humorist who knew him well was Rabelais, who lectured on him and edited him along with Hippocrates in 1532. It is piquant to observe that all this enthusiasm could coexist with a hospital director, who, if we may believe Tzetzes, *Ep.* 81, ed. Leone 121, did not even know Galen's dates. The *Timarion*'s epi-

thet for Galen is paralleled by earlier Byzantine commentators such as John Philoponus and Simplicius, who dub him "the most learned," "the marvelous," and so on. After all this, it is almost a relief to encounter Wilamowitz' dismissal of him as *Seichbeutel* ("windbag"). Psellus' contemporary Simeon Seth, *Controversy with Galen* 44, ed. Daremberg, has sarcastic remarks about those who call Galen divine; cf. Temkin, *DOP* 16 (1962), 108. The author may be reflecting this debate. The reference to Galen in the *Timarion* may be to a new edition of the work in question currently published or promised in Constantinople. As Temkin, *DOP* 16 (1962), 115, says, the joke may be that Galen is contemplating revisions that would result in a volume even bigger than the verbose original. An artistic reason for his absence from the medical conclave may be the need to preserve the trinity of experts, which then balances the 3 judges and the 3 scholars who make up the courtroom officials in ch. 44.

174. A place that makes us think of errant schoolboys, which is precisely where they are located in *Philogelos* 61. There is no indication in Romano that the verb *engoniazo* is in any way uncommon, although it is not in *LSJ* or Lampe; Stephanus has a few patristic and Byzantine parallels.

175. There is a similar jingle in the Greek.

176. Their infernal status is seen in terms of Byzantine promotion.

177. It was no doubt this implied defence of religious freedom that helped to earn the author his denunciation by Constantine Acropolites.

178. Again, notice the term "Galilaean," also the cool attitude towards Christianity's triumph.

179. Theophilus (819–42), the son of Michael II, was the last of the iconoclast emperors. Despite this, he gets a generally good press from the orthodox sources such as George the Monk, Genesius, Theophanes Continuatus, and Nicetas; cf. Ellissen's note, also Constantelos 114 for references and for discussion of his charitable works. Modern historians tend to agree; cf. Ostrogorsky, *His-*

tory of the Byzantine State, 206–7. Romano adduces Lucian, *True Story* 2. 10, to suggest that he is here couched in terms of the proverbial Athenian democrat, Aristides the Just. Ostrogorsky compares him to the famous caliph Harun al Rashid for going around the city to ascertain and correct his subjects' grievances. This was something the early Athenian tyrant Peisistratus had done, so also (though hostile sources pervert the motive into a quest after low life) Roman emperors such as Nero. Theophilus, then, combines many images. Diehl, *Seminarium Kondakovianum* 4 (1931), 37 is worth quoting here: "A la justice de Trajan la justice de Theophile fait pendant. L'Occident catholique a, pour sa justice, pardonné à Trajan son paganisme et l'a fait monter de l'enfer au paradis chrétien. L'Orient orthodoxe a, pour sa justice, pardonné à Théophile son hérésie et ses cruautés et l'a fait lui aussi, asseoir au paradis." Diehl is here alluding to Trajan's promotion by Dante. The Italian poet, incidentally, includes only one Byzantine emperor, Justinian, *Parad.* 6. 1. f.—in *Inf.* 4. 129 he juxtaposes Saladin with classical heroes, which would not be to Byzantine taste. Nevertheless, it may still be puzzling that the iconoclast emperor should retain his high standing in the period of the Comneni, whose strict orthodoxy is a major theme of Anna's history. There is, in fact, a less favourable allusion to Theophilus in Nicolas Mesarites, ed. Downey 40. 8–9, where the emperor is said to have belched forth the venom of impiety against the holy images and to have poured it over those who venerated them; he goes on to recall Theophilus' branding of iconodule monks with insulting verses. This, combined with the obtruded claim of our author that he had gotten his impression of Theophilus from the historians, may hint at a contemporary controversy.

180. Romano designates the Green *aperiskopon* as late, giving no parallel. Stephanus adduces only this passage; *LSJ* has only the adverbial form, from Tzetzes.

181. The *locus amoenus,* or "oasis of delight," is a commonplace in classical and mediaeval literature; cf. Curtius, *European Literature and the Latin Middle Ages,* 192 f.

On the Byzantine side, see also Littlewood, *BMGS* 5 (1979), 95–114. In the present context, it is best to recall Lucian, *True Story* 2. 5, and Dante, *Inf.* 4. 111. The Garden of Eden will naturally be thought of in Christian Byzantium. With regard to the *Timarion,* it is also worth noting a paradise garden scene from a mosaic in the Thessalonica church of St Demetrius. For such interrelations between art and literature, cf. Maguire, *Art and Eloquence in Byzantium.* Reality may also be an element. The description of the royal palace Philopation by Cinnamus 2. 14. 74–75 (*PG* 133. 396C) is somewhat reminiscent; being a satirist, our author could conceivably intend a subtle allusion to imperial luxury.

182.   This aspect also has a strong literary pedigree, with parallels in Homer, pseudo-Plato, *Axiochus* 371D, and Lucian, *True Story* 2. 5. Spring rather than summer is a classical rather than Californian notion of eternal bliss. Given the summers in Constantinople, it makes sense. So also in Italy, where Vergil, *Georgics* 2. 149, visualised a paradise of *ver adsiduum.* Theodore Prodromos, *Ep.* 1 (*PG* 133. 1239A) quotes the proverbial one swallow does not make a spring, whereas we of course say summer. For spring in Byzantine literature and art, cf. Maguire, *Art and Eloquence in Byzantium,* 43 f.

183.   Why have they only now come to court, more than a thousand years later? Is the backup of cases in Hades as chronic as it is in modern courts? Cf. the introduction for Romano's notion that we have here a delicate allusion to the murder of John II Comnenus in 1143, with obvious consequences for the dating of the *Timarion.* As always, the literary element must not be overlooked. Lucian, *True Story* 2. 2, also has his narrator stand in line for justice, although in this instance the verdicts on the 3 cases ahead of him are recorded; cf. *Menippus or The Descent into Hell* 13. Dante, *Inf.* 34. 61 f. (cf. *Parad.* 6. 74), puts Brutus and Cassius along with Judas Iscariot in the lowest reaches of hell. The *Timarion's* attitude is in marked contrast with Theodore Prodromos, *Ep.* 5 (*PG* 133. 1253), where Brutus and Cassius, along with the younger Cato, are held up as models of

principled courage for their suicides; cf. *Ep* 8 (*PG* 133. 1273A), in which Brutus, along with Cato (which one is unclear) and Caesar, is named as one of the great orators of old Rome. These Byzantine references are not in the *Nachleben* of Brutus assembled by M. L. Clarke, *Brutus, the Noblest Roman*, 79 f.

184. My version here accepts the addition of the second *su* ("you") to the text by Hase, followed by Ellissen and Romano. The iteration is artistically appropriate, and the word is so close to its first occurrence that it could easily have been missed out by the scribe.

185. The Greek *misodikaios* is registered in no lexicon and might be the author's invention. For the similar compounds *misomartys* and *misostephanos*, also unnoticed by lexica, see the texts edited by Papageorgiu, *BZ* 12 (1903), 259.

186. It is typical of Theodore that he should think gluttony an argument in favour of his client. Since this item was not part of the narrator's earlier account, the reader must have been supposed to assume either that it had been disclosed in conversation between their meeting and the present moment, or that Theodore is the sort of unscrupulous advocate who invents "evidence." The Greek word *alektoris* was defined as a poetic or Hellenistic term by the 2nd-century A.D. lexicographers Phrynichus, ed. Rutherford 228, and Pollux, *Onomasticon* 2. 15. It is dubbed a fake atticism by Browning, *Byzantinobulgarica* 1 (1962), 291, where its occurrence in correspondence between Michael Italicus and Theodore Prodromos gains interest in the light of both authors' claims to the *Timarion*. But the word is not all that uncommon or pretentious in late Greek, being (for easy instance) twice on display in the anonymous treatise *On Food*, ed. *PMGM* 259. 15, 17.

187. As in ch. 37, this must be the meaning of *soudarion* (originally a loan word from the Latin *sudarium*) here, although elsewhere in late Greek (e.g. Ducas, *Hist.* 39. 20) it seems to mean veil; cf. Wilson 154. The author may intend to dig at Byzantine fashions here: the late historian Nicephorus Gregoras complained of young dandies

coming to church in Persian hats and Italian dresses, or the reverse; cf. Laiou-Thomadakis, *DOP* 34–35 (1980–1), 186. In the very unreliable *Patria Cpoleos,* ed. Preger 1. 83, Justinian is said to have worn a *soudarion* whilst inspecting the progress on the building of St Sophia. The *Timarion's* attitude to such headgear may support the disbelief in this item evinced by Mango, *Byzantium and the Classical Tradition,* 51. Interestingly in the present condition, the noun entered Armenian as a loan word; cf. Thumb, *BZ* 9 (1900), 419.

188. The meaning is not in doubt, but the Greek merits a brief comment. The one manuscript has the adjectival form *melaneimoni,* which Hase altered to the cognate verb *emelaneimonei,* a change favoured by Macleod in his *JHS* review of Romano. Romano himself, following Tode, prints the noun *melaneimonia.* On artistic grounds, this may be the best, since it yields a tricolon of nouns, although the verb would make a pair with the one immediately preceding. The noun is found in Nicetas Choniates, *Hist.* 500. 88, where the editor van Dieten denotes it as unique. It is worth noting that Michael Italicus has the adjective in the aforementioned letter (note 186), and the verb in *Ep.* 23. As Tozer, *JHS* 2 (1881), 253, observes, contemporary accounts of Theophilus do not mention this characteristic. It would naturally suit his image of the selfless man of justice; we have earlier seen that Psellus tends to equate imperial virtue with sartorial austerity. On the other hand, it is always possible that the author has invented the detail, either to remind his audience of the black-robed Furies of Aeschylus, or simply as a contrast with the white radiance of his guardian angel.

189. For *lampros* used of bodily appearance, Romano adduces Herodotus 4. 64, which is probably unnecessary in light of Psellus, *Chron.* 3. 19: *lampro chromati* ("shining skin").

190. Romano does not notice Lucian, *Lover of Lies* 25 (cf. note 99), where the narrator encounters a similar figure in his infernal adventure. The author's compound *leukendytes* is unique to this passage, according to Stephanus—Romano wrongly notes it as absent from all lexica.

191. Tozer, *JHS* 2 (1881), 253, calls this a profane and unorthodox allusion; Constantelos, *Byzantine Philanthropy and Social Welfare*, 60, sees it as ridiculing the notion of divine emperors. Romano has no comment at all. In fact, the idea of a guardian angel, apart from reminding the reader of Socrates' famous *daemon*, seems well grounded in biblical and patristic thought. Ellissen adduced Matthew 18. 10 and Revelations 15. 12 from the New Testament; cf. Lampe for patristic passages. The belief is discussed and demonstrated at length by Brown, *The Cult of Saints*, 50–68.

192. One of the defending devils makes a similarly stentorian opening in ch. 39, and Theodore himself will also be found booming away again later. There may be an allusion to contemporary forensic style, although jokes about loud orators are as old as Periclean Athens.

193. Tozer, *JHS* 2 (1881), 253, renders the names as Speedy and Nightspy. Parody of legal procedure is at least as old as the *Wasps* of Aristophanes. The author's model is clearly Lucian, who makes much use of the device; cf. Householder, *TAPA* 71 (1940), 199–216. As far as I can see, he makes little or no use of Demosthenes and company. This would also seem to be the impression of Romano, whose notes identify no quotations or echoes of the orators, apart from a possible reminiscence of Isaeus in ch. 39. For another Byzantine parody, cf. the "Mafia" text edited by Hunger, *RESE* 7 (1969), 95–107, where the welter of made-up names includes a Nyktibios (Nightrider).

194. More repetition (cf. note 160) but defensible this time, since the judges have to be given the evidence.

195. I have translated the reading *astrabelatountos*, adopted by Ellissen and Romano from Hase's certain emendation of the manuscript *astrabe lalountos*, albeit the verb thus created is otherwise unattested and is in no lexicon. The author was probably aiming for a variant on the noun *astrabelates* in his likely source, Lucian, *Lexiphanes* 2.

196. My "firmly rooted . . . brutally" reflects a similar play on sound and meaning in the Greek adverbs *bebaios . . . biaios*.

Notes

197. Minos' very unprofessional jumping to conclusions will remind the modern reader of the Queen of Hearts in *Alice in Wonderland*.

198. Who will, however, join in their final defence in 38. Nyktion is here described by the adjective *lamyros,* which has already been used (23) to describe Theodore, and which will be used again (39). Small touches like this help to give us some respect for the author's artistic capabilities. In his opening remarks, Nyktion makes one think again of the Furies, arguably the author's intention.

199. This adjective shows that Nyktion had been listening closely to what Timarion had told Theodore in ch. 25.

200. The Greek *tauta eipon ekeinoi* is plural, although only Nyktion has spoken. No editor has commented, much less changed it to the singular. Carelessness by the author is possible; so is scribal error, since the very next paragraph begins (correctly, with regard to the judges) *tauta eipon.* Cf. ch. 38, where the conductors' joint speech is postluded by *tauta elegon.* In either case it would be understandable, given that Nyktion uses the plural throughout his address, to associate Oxybas in the defence. Perhaps the author intends us to think of a chorus in Greek Tragedy, where one individual can speak for all. Or we may be meant to imagine Oxybas as nodding and mumbling assent to his partner's arguments. Compare ch. 46 (note 249), where one of the ushers goes mysteriously missing.

201. The Greek adjective *leukophos* appears in no lexicon; Hase altered it to *lykophos* on the basis of the contemporary Eustathius 689. 21. Romano signals the noun *augasma* as late, giving no example; it occurs in, e.g., l. 500 of David Dishypatos' poem on Akindynos, ed. Browning *B* 27 (1957), 713–45.

202. Something that may have been on Timarion's mind, in view of the fate of Romanus Diogenes.

203. A precise source is hardly needed for so simple a detail, yet there is a certain reminiscence of Lucian, *Lexiphanes* 2.

204. Saffron-robed Dawn comes from *Il.* 8. 1; 24. 695; cf. *Od.* 2. 1, also exploited by Heliodorus 3. 4. In the next

sentence, the doctors are introduced in the phraseology of *Il.* 1. 253; 4. 1.

205. The 3-day period might be a conscious reflection of that between the Passion and Resurrection of Christ, something that would suit the *Timarion's* subtitle, "The story of his sufferings" (*pathematon*). But this is a suspiciously frequent phenomenon in Byzantine historiography: both sacks of Constantinople (1204, 1453) are said to have lasted 3 days, as did the Arab looting of Thessalonica in 904.

206. Romano does not comment on the Greek *orthopages,* although the only other example furnished by lexica is Plutarch's essay on the bravery of Alexander (*Moralia* 340C), used of a headdress (*kidaris*) and so possibly the author's inspiration here. Cf. Xenophon, *Anabasis* 2. 5. 53, where the *orthe* tiara is said to be the king's monopoly.

207. This section is particularly rich in Lucianic pastiche, but we should not overlook (as does Romano) the contemporary elements. Tonsure, for notable instance, was the Byzantine prelude to entering a monastery, and this was often forcibly inflicted on a prominent individual of whom the authorities wished to be rid without the more odious penalty of blinding. Romano does not discuss the author's noun *apokarsis,* although it is absent from *LSJ.* Other lexica identify it as patristic; for a Byzantine secular example, cf. Psellus, *Chron.* 4. 52, describing the (voluntary) tonsure of Michael IV.

208. Just as the judges had done in ch. 35, where the same splendid verb *hypopsithyrizo* (cf. note 66) is employed.

209. Most of their speech, reasonably enough within this legal framework, is a rehash of earlier sections.

210. There could here be an echo of the description of mummification procedures in Herodotus 2. 86, one of which involved hooking out the brain via the nostrils.

211. Again. This is now the third time we have had this description.

212. A natural enough thing for the rival advocate to say, but the author may intend, in view of his Greek *adikon rhetoreian,* a recollection of the Unjust Cause in Aristophanes' *Clouds;* cf. the next note.

213. Stephanus gives no other example of the Greek *stomphastes,* and neither *LSJ* nor Lampe acknowledge it. Romano thinks the author coined it on the model of the verb *stomphazo* in Aristophanes, *Wasps* 721. I would prefer to think that (instead or as well) he had in mind the noun *stomphax* at *Clouds* 1367, since that would strengthen the point made in the previous note about his sources. For cognate rarities, cf. the Homeric commentaries of Eustathius 12. 4 (significantly with *onkos,* a favourite image of our author, as we have seen); 1123. 41; 1350. 24.

214. What follows is a paraphrase of information already given, though cf. the introduction for the possible significance of the imperial patronage of Theodore.

215. The word *threskeumon* occurs only here according to Stephanus who indeed alters it to *-ma,* something no editor of the *Timarion* has done; other lexica do not notice the word. Given the preceding *-on* and the following *-o* in the Greek, a scribe could very well have made such a mistake.

216. Romano adduces the 4th-century B.C. orator Isaeus 2. 37, where 3rd and 9th day feasts are in fact mentioned in honour of the deceased. But this is largely beside the Byzantine point. The operative source is pseudo-Macarius, *On the Fate of Souls* (*PG* 34. 388), where obsequies on the 3rd, 9th, and 40th days, said to be a tradition, are prescribed. The point of these prayers was to help the soul of the departed find the best lodging place possible until the Last Judgement. In some quarters, it was thought that the soul could revisit earth until the 40th day, was shown the delights of heaven and the torments of hell, and after due obeisance to God was assigned a place of residence. The lodgings of the characters Timarion first meets in Hades look reminiscent of this belief, and he does get a sample of paradise, although (as will be seen) there is very little hell fire or torment in the piece.

217. I agree with Romano in rejecting the notion of Hase, followed by Ellissen, that there is a gap in the text here. It is rather a dramatic aposiopesis or falling silent for effect.

218. The Greek is *euoptos,* uniquely employed here in this
sense according to Romano. But see Pollux 2. 51, a
reference given doubtfully by Stephanus who did not
notice the *Timarion* passage. The adjective might have
this sense in its two appearances (1. 197; 4. 54) in the
Hodoiporikon of Constantine Manasses, both times as
one of a string of compliments to a lovely girl; however,
it may mean no more than "good to look at."
219. Nicely rendered Sharpeye and Nightspy by Tozer, *JHS* 2
(1881), 254.
220. Romano detects an allusion to John 19. 34, the blood
and water that issue from the crucified Christ. But we
may not need to look beyond Lucian, *True Story* 2. 46,
for the source.
221. The manuscript reading is *kyamois* ("beans," that is
"votes," according to classical Greek practice). Hase
emended to *kemois,* literally meaning the funnel-shaped
tops of voting urns, an emendation adopted by Ellissen
and favoured though not printed by Romano. This may
well be right, but the tautology could be mitigated by
taking *kyamois* in the sense of "lots," a natural extension of meaning.
222. The Greek genitive plural in the manuscript yields an
otherwise unattested noun *eisangelos.* There is no obvious
reason why the author should want to invent a new word
for such an ordinary notion, especially as we have seen
that he is not addicted to neologisms. Hence Hase may
well be right in emending to *-eon,* producing the regular
eisangeleus; Ellissen, but not Romano, follows him.
223. Aristarchus was one of the most celebrated and strict of
the Alexandrian scholars of the 3rd and 2nd centuries
B.C. who were particularly noted for their work on the
text and interpretation of Homer. The best account of
him is Pfeiffer, *History of Classical Scholarship,* 210–33.
224. Along with the earlier compliment to his extempore
skills, it is the Greek verb *hypopsellizon* used here for
whispering that is the basis for equating this Byzantine
Professor with Michael Psellus; cf. Dräseke, *BZ* 6
(1897), 483–90. The allusive pun is certainly in the author's manner. For the verb itself, *LSJ* cites only the

Notes

4th-century A.D. orator and epistolographer Libanius, *Oration* 43. 21; Lampe furnishes some patristic examples. Romano denotes it as late, giving no parallel. There is one in Nicephorus Basilaces, *Preface to His Own Book* 13, ed. Garzya. Theodore Prodromos, *Plato-Lover* 5. 12, has the cognate *hypopsello*. Anna Comnena 1. 8 says her father was abused by Basilacius as "the lisper"; cf. the jokes in 5th-century Athens about the inability of Alcibiades to pronounce the *r* sound. It is impossible in a summary to do justice to the many-sided talents of Michael Psellus. He has been compared to Roger Bacon and Albertus Magnus, also to Voltaire which is patently absurd; cf. Barker, *Social and Political Thought in Byzantium from Justinian to the Last Palaeologus,* 131. The most useful account in the present context is probably that of Hussey, *Church and Learning in the Byzantine Empire 867–1185,* esp. 37–50, 61–88; cf. Ostrogorsky, *History of the Byzantine State,* 327 f. (with extensive bibliography). For the future, readers should keep an eye open for the work being done on him by two distinguished scholars, John Duffy and Kenneth Snipes. Briefly, Psellus was born in 1018 of a noble but not rich family. His early years were something of a struggle, but thanks to his mother's acumen he was fortunate in his tutor and fellow pupils: John Mauropous, later archbishop of Euchaita; the future emperor Constantine X Ducas; the statesman Lichudes; and John Xiphilinus, first president of the refounded university of Constantinople in 1045, later patriarch. Psellus eventually ascended to the chair of rhetoric, holding the title consul of the philosophers. A wily and not always attractive personality, he was an influential courtier under various emperors until abandoned by Michael VII, his former pupil. Psellus fades out after this blow, apparently dying c. 1078. As is so often the case with Byzantine authors, many of his writings are not yet available in modern editions, much less in translation. Readers of the *Timarion* will get most enjoyment and profit from his *Chronography;* cf. the Bibliography for details. Highly personal, often distorted (as we saw in the case of Romanus Diogenes), it is one of the liveliest works in Byzantine literature. Two of Psellus' most manifest characteristics (here he resembles Cicero) are his vanity and his satirical wit. Those who read Greek can sample the latter in the form of his long and abusive iambic poem against Jacob the Monk, ed. Sternbach, *WS* 25 (1903), 10–39.

225. Romano has no note here, but this looks to me like a parody of the Homeric formula whereby words break the barrier of the speaker's teeth.

226. Phrynichus was one of the best known and most pedantic critics and lexicographers of the 2nd century A.D. Byzantine interest in him is exemplified by Photius' summary, *Bibliotheca,* cod. 158, of his *Sophistic Preparation.* Although a Byzantine damning prolixity may seem like the pot calling the kettle black, it is good to see Photius criticising the verbosity of the work, which he thought should be cut by at least a fifth, and also laughing at the inelegant style of one purporting to teach good writing to others. Cf. the lighthearted reference to Phrynichus in Michael Italicus, *Ep.* 1. An abridged lexicon, *Ecloge,* ed. Rutherford, survives, in which Phrynichus dogmatically and often inaccurately attempts to settle what is correct Attic style and what is not. This sort of thing—one will nowadays think of John Simon's *Paradigms Lost* (London, 1980)—was effectively satirised by Lucian and strongly criticised by Galen. There is a good thumbnail sketch of Phrynichus in the *Oxford Classical Dictionary,* 2nd ed., 829–30.

227. This formulation is a parody of the typical decree of the Athenian Assembly, being part and parcel of the sustained legal humour; cf. note 193.

228. The inspiration for this is Lucian, *Lover of Lies* 25, where the narrator is acquitted by Pluto who is angry at the conductor for bringing him down to Hades prematurely.

229. *Il.* 2. 1–2. Romano does not observe that the author owes his parody to Lucian, *Icaromenippus* 28, and *Twice Accused* 2. Anna Comnena has a partial quotation of it at 1. 6, the full version in 7. 11.

230. These are all pre-Socratic thinkers, celebrated for their interest in science and logic. Others who might have been named include Xenophanes, Heraclitus, Anaximenes, Empedocles, Democritus, and Zeno. For texts and translations, cf. Kirk and Raven, *The PreSocratic Philosophers*. The absence of Socrates, Plato, Aristotle, and the later Stoics and Epicureans is notable. In Dante's circle of philosophers (*Inf.* 4. 130 f.), Aristotle presides over a group that includes Anaxagoras (inventor of the idea of an Intelligence or *Nous* presiding over the universe) and Thales (commonly regarded as the first scientist in Greek thought). Diogenes (on whom see below) and Galen are only passing names. To what extent the pre-Socratics were any more than names to our author is uncertain. He could just be showing off, an all too typical element of Byzantine writing. Kirk and Raven point out that, apart from the odd mention in such polymaths as Tzetzes, the fragments of their works come from authors not later than the 6th-century philosophy commentator Simplicius. None of them feature in Photius, who indeed includes only 6 authors (4 orators, 2 historians) from the 5th century, and none from any earlier time; cf. Treadgold, *The Nature of the Bibliotheca of Photius*. Yet one contemporary of the *Timarion* whose knowledge may have been more than superficial was Michael Italicus, whose correspondence is studded with their names and who devotes an entire letter (*Ep.* 18) to Empedocles. Theodore Prodromos also sprinkles his letters with their names.

231. Diogenes is, of course, the famous Cynic philosopher who lived in a "tub" (actually, a huge amphora or wine cask) in Athens in the 4th century B.C. His maverick views on morality and rough way of handling contemporaries (e.g. telling Alexander the Great to get out of his light, an episode tactfully alluded to in ch. 44) attracted a fund of anecdote; cf. Dudley, *A History of Cynicism*. Together with his successor Menippus, he is a natural hero in the satires of Lucian, one reason for his presence here. The author makes him sound like a savage dog, which naturally suits his label (Cynic equals "doglike" in Greek).

232. There is a considerable modern literature on this fascinating character, the most recent study being Clucas,
*The Trial of John Italus and the Crisis of Intellectual
Values in Byzantium in the Eleventh Century.* See also
Hussey, *Church and Learning in the Byzantine Empire
867–1185,* 90–94; Browning, *PP* 69 (1975), 3–23. The
contemporary documents of church and court relating
the trial and anathematised beliefs of John were published by Uspenskij, *IRAIC* 2 (1897), 1–66. There is a
detailed account in Anna Comnena 5. 8, inevitably
spiteful and hostile since her imperial father was so involved in the impeachment. Briefly, John Italus came
from southern Italy (hence his name), the son of a Norman. These foreign origins and concomitant poor Greek
accent are grist to the mill of his opponents' cruel humour. He came to Constantinople around 1050, and was
a student of Psellus, whom he succeeded as consul of the
philosophers. He first got into trouble for "impiety"
around 1076, but the case against him was abortive. The
axe fell in 1082, significantly soon after the accession of
Alexius I. A tribunal composed of both lay and church
figures judged him to be dangerously heretical and pagan, labels that could mean as little then as those of
"bourgeois" and "fascist" in Communist jargon. John
was anathematised, banned from teaching, and fades
out of our sight, hence we do not know when he died. It
is commonly said that he ended his days in a monastery;
cf. Browning, *PP* 69 (1975), 15. However, Anna 5. 9,
wrapping up the episode, says that John lived on for
quite a while (*en hysterois kairois*), and was known to
have changed his mind and to be attempting to revise his
Platonism to fit the orthodox pieties. Clearly then, he
had not dropped out of contemporary sight. We do not
know the whole story. As has often been pointed out,
he was the first intellectual (heretic churchmen apart) to
be condemned for his teaching since the 6th-century
crackdown by Justinian. Personal issues seemed to have
played at least as important a role as ideological ones,
though the *Timarion* stresses the latter, and, as Anna
Comnena shows, the age was one of religious ferment,

what with Nilus and his reformed monophysitism, the Blachernites and the Enthusiasts, the Bogomils, and so on; cf. Runciman, *The Medieval Manichee,* 70.

233. Romano does not comment on the Greek *hemiandrion,* although it is not in *LSJ.* Earlier editions of Liddell and Scott give Theophylact Simocatta, *Ep.* 43 (ed. Hercher), which is also the only passage adduced by Stephanus. Theophylact uses the word of a eunuch; cf. Lucian, *Council of the Gods* 23, for the cognate *hemiandros.*

234. Romano follows Hase and Ellissen in connecting this character with Theodore Prodromos, the contemporary jack of all literary trades whose satrical and other writings have been so frequently alluded to in these notes. Any such equation makes evident nonsense of Hunger's notion (cf. the Introduction) that Prodromos might actually have been the author of the *Timarion.* But I can see no good reason for the identification. There is no obvious detail which would seem to give the sort of clue furnished by the author for his earlier introductions of such subsidiary characters, of which the present one may indeed be simply a doublet. For instance, if we are to take the opening salvo literally, Prodromos is not known to have been unusually small. Pockmarked would have been a different proposition, in view of his sufferings from smallpox; cf. note 87. It would have been easy for the author to provide a punning clue on his name, as earlier with Palaeologus and Psellus. Both of Theodore Prodromos' names, meaning respectively "Gift of God" and "Forerunner," lend themselves conveniently to wordplay. He could easily have been introduced as running before John Italus rather than behind. Incidentally, no proponent of the identification has produced any reason to suppose that Prodromos was in any sense a follower of Italus, which is the natural implication of the author's words. Much has been made of the reference to his abusive iambic poems, with Romano 144 following Garzya's suggestion, *BS* 34 (1973), 8, n. 33, that Michael Italicus might allude to Prodromos as one of the *andraria* and *iambeiophagoi* mentioned in a speech to John II Comnenus. But this ignores the fact that Mi-

chael and Prodromos were on good terms; cf. Browning, *Byzantinobulgarica* 1 (1962), 279–97; Papadimitriou, *Feodor Prodromos: Istoriko-literature izsledovanie;* Michael Italicus, *Ep.* 14. In any case, the accusation is a standard one, with a literary pedigree extending back to Demosthenes, *On the Crown* 139. The chronicler Scylitzes (p. 785 Bonn-*PG* 122. 856D) ridicules the iambic effusions of Michael VII; cf. the war of the iambic pamphlets between Constantine the Rhodian and Theodore the Paphlagonian eunuch, ed. Matranga, *Anecdota Graeca* 2. 624–32. In general, the author's description is commonplace both in content (for a parallel, see Agathias' account, *Hist.* 2. 29. 1. f., of the alleged tub-thumping quack Uranius in Justinian's time) and language—Romano's own notes show it to be full of tags from Aristophanes.

235. A proverbial expression, as Ellissen and Romano notice, though neither scholar traces it back to the earliest source, the poet Archilochus, fr. 110. Ellissen, but not Romano, also noted it in Lucian, *The Fake Sophist* 32.

236. A stock in trade of the Cynics, but there may be something of a pun, since the Greek *atapeinotos* can also mean "invincible" in late Greek; cf. Lampe for patristic examples.

237. My "dog . . . dogma" version reflects a similar wordplay in the Greek.

238. Anna Comnena confirms that John's violent temper would sometimes make him resort to physical assault on opponents.

239. Presumably Cato the Censor, the Roman Republic's version of John Bull or Uncle Sam, notorious for his dislike of philosophers and other "fancy foreign things," rather than the equally celebrated Cato the Younger, who killed himself at Utica in Africa rather than live to see Julius Caesar triumphant. If so, add the *Timarion* passage to Schmitt, *Klio* 48 (1967), 325–34. Psellus, *Chron.* 7. 75, uses the censor as a paradigm of fortitude in sickness. The younger Cato is featured in Dante, *Purg.* 1. 31 f. Theodore Prodromos uses him more than once in his letters (e.g. *Ep.* 8) as a moral exemplar.

240. This oath must be meant to remind the reader of Socrates' famous imprecation "By the Dog."

241. The Greek *sophistorhetor* is very rare (Romano indicates it to be late, giving no parallel), elsewhere only in the contemporary Tzetzes, *Hist.* 11. 189, and so possibly a cant term in the intellectual quarrels of the age.

242. Why does John run to Aristotle rather than Plato? Perhaps only because of the superior sound effects of the former's name. But the allusion could be more serious. John is anathematised for his Platonising doctrines, hence Aristotle, who was thought more scientifically useful (cf. his later invocation in the West against Galileo) and less dangerous than Plato, would be the logical refuge; cf. Meyendorff, *Byzantine Theology,* 63–65. The respective merits of Plato and Aristotle could cause sharp controversy, such as that between Psellus and Xiphilinus; cf. Hussey, *Church and Learning in the Byzantine Empire 867–1185,* 46–47.

243. Romano has nothing to say about the Greek *choiremporos,* albeit outside the inscriptions and papyri adduced by *LSJ* it seems unique to this passage. Not that the style of insult is rare—quite the contrary. In the aforementioned iambic exchange with Theodore the Paphlagonian (cf. note 234), also in his similar attacks on Leo Choirosphactes, Constantine the Rhodian deals out many porcine pasquinades, notably (in the present contact) *choiropaphlagon.* In *Mazaris* 150, a character is ridiculed as "the pig *soupasis* (a Turkish official)," which discloses that this sort of thing comports racial and religious prejudice; it was one way of suggesting that the victim was a Jew or Turk. A sexual connotation is also possible, since the author and his readers will have been aware of the famous scene in the *Acharnians* of Aristophanes, where there is an extended sequence of puns depending upon the colloquial sense of vagina for *choiros*. This *double entendre* is certainly understood in the ridicule of the pig-like life (*choirobios*) of the ephemeral emperor Alexander (912) in Theophanes Continuatus 6. 2 (*PG* 109. 379D). The sense is preserved in the modern vulgarism "to pork." It would be nice to think that our author was

aware of the incident in Paris on October 1, 1131, in which a runaway pig caused a French prince to have a fatal fall from horseback, thereby provoking instant legislation against stray hogs. I owe this delicious item to Soyer, *The Pantropheion,* 141, a history of food in antiquity from which readers of the *Timarion* with its accent on gluttony would derive pleasure and profit.

244. Paphlagonians are also abused in the final chapter. For a near contemporary defence of them, perhaps alluding to Michael IV (1034–41), who came from Paphlagonia, cf. a scholiast on Lucian, *Alexander the False Prophet* 22. One distinguished son of Paphlagonia was Psellus' teacher and future archbishop, John Mauropous (cf. note 224). Like Cappadocians, Paphlagonians are proverbial butts of humour; cf. Jeffries, *DOP* 28 (1974), 160, citing a reference by Arethas to Paphlagonians who knocked on doors, sang, and demanded money in the style of Halloween or Christmas carol singers. But the word can be a nuisance, since it is often applied as a non-ethnic insult in the sense of "windbag," on the model of Aristophanes' attacks on the demagogue Cleon in his *Knights.* On the error this once produced in e.g. the case of the late Roman poet Claudian, cf. Alan Cameron, *Claudian,* 3, 245.

245. Psellus in one way does not suit this situation, in that he regarded philosophy and rhetoric as mutually good and complementary; cf. Barker, *Social and Political Theory in Byzantium,* 132, for translations of some relevant extracts. Perhaps it is partly the pretensions of Psellus himself—not noted for humility—that are being laughed at. But the sequence also reflects the mutual jealousies and rivalries between the intellectuals of the day, exacerbated as they were by the John Italus affair. Italus himself pursued his philosophy at the expense of rhetorical style which in the words of Mango, *Byzantium: The Empire of New Rome,* 145, made him a new phenomenon on the Byzantine intellectual scene. Presumably as a reaction, the Church now attempted to influence education by creating a network of secular and religious schools forming overall the so-called Patriarchal School.

For a detailed account of its syllabus, from which philosophy was apparently excluded, and personnel, cf. Browning, *B* 32 (1962), 167–201; *B* 33 (1963), 11–40. Significantly, a church-sponsored master of rhetoric is first attested in 1082, the very year of John Italus' condemnation. Another reflection of this changed situation is the comparison between rhetoric and philosophy, to the former's benefit, by Michael Italicus, *Ep.* 2.

246. The Greek both here and at the chapter's end is full of technical terms from rhetorical theory, mostly inherited from such classical writers as Aristotle, Demetrius, Dionysius of Halicarnassus, Longinus, Menander Rhetor, and above all the 2nd-century Hermogenes of Tarsus, on whose arid texts the Byzantines (e.g. Tzetzes, Gregory of Corinth, John the Logothete—all around the 12th century) were forever producing commentaries, a significant reflection of their taste. For a general appreciation, cf. Kennedy, *Classical Rhetoric and Its Christian and Secular Tradition from Ancient to Modern Times,* 161–72; Maguire, *Art and Eloquence in Byzantium.* More detailed is Kustas, *Studies in Byzantine Rhetoric.* For a flood of technicalities similar to the one here, cf. Michael Italicus, *Ep.* 29.

247. Thanks to the author, too much has been made of this as a feature of Psellan style and flattery. Comparison of an emperor to the sun was a trope recommended by Menander Rhetor back in the 3rd century, *On Epideictic Oratory* 378. 10 f. For its persistence and frequency, both in late Roman and Byzantine panegyric, cf. MacCormack, *Art and Ceremony in Late Antiquity,* 20; Kantarowicz, *DOP* 17 (1963), 161, citing for instance an example from the verse panegyrics of Theodore Prodromos. There is a perhaps significant plethora of examples from the Comnenan period: Michael Italicus devotes the whole of *Ep.* 23 to the conceit, beginning with the statement that he himself thus addresses the emperor, as indeed he does in *Epp.* 6, 29; an alphabetic address to Alexius I by Stephanos Physopalamites, ed. Walz, *Anecdota Byzantina,* 52–55, has it in the opening line; see also Constantine Manasses, *Hodoiporikon* 4. 135. With

regard to Romano's theory of the *Timarion*'s authorship, it is interesting to find it in Nicolas Callicles 25. 36.
Alexius I is the Eastern Sun in 1. 9 of an anonymous
speech addressed to him, ed. Browning, *B* 28 (1958),
31–50. When Browning asks if this Eastern reference
has any significance for the emperor's movements on
campaign, the answer is probably no, in view of the
foregoing examples.

248. Three big names from the so-called Second Sophistic
movement in the 2nd century A.D.; they feature with
many more of their kind in Philostratus, *Lives of the
Sophists*. The best general account is Bowersock, *Greek
Sophists in the Roman Empire*. Polemo of Laodicea (c.
88–145) wrote typical declamations on classical themes,
also a treatise on physiognomy which survives in an
Arabic version. Herodes Atticus (c. 107–77) was one of
the richest men of his time, an ancient Rockefeller
whose benefactions to Athens can still be appreciated in
the form of his building work. He was consul in 143, and
enjoyed the confidence of emperors; cf. Graindor, *Un
milliardaire antique: Hérode Atticus et sa famille*. Aelius
Aristides (c. 129–89) is unusual in that a large number
of his speeches have survived, presumably a tribute to
his later popularity. Their most notable feature is his
lifelong hypochondria (Galen himself comments on it)
and the sometimes extraordinary remedies prescribed
by Aesculapius, whose low position in the *Timarion*'s
Hades he would not have appreciated. Suffering and
insufferable to many, Aristides has earned a detailed
and sympathetic study by Behr, *Aelius Aristides and the
Sacred Tales*.

249. The Greek for "dusk to dawn" is the otherwise unattested compound *hesperorthrion*. Notice here also, and
later in the chapter, that one of the two ushers has apparently gone missing.

250. This looks like a flippant allusion to the Resurrection of
Christ, though Romano has no comment. If so, it would
be another item that earned the satire the condemnation
of Constantine Acropolites.

251. The author is here possibly drawing on Lucian, *True*

Story 2. 29, where Odysseus sends a secret letter to Calypso by the narrator.

252. Oddly enough, the Greek word *ornithopoles* seems to occur elsewhere only in Pollux 7. 198, though one imagines it must have been frequent in literature and life.

253. Theodore's shopping list contains several items (hens, lamb, sucking pigs) that were often regarded as luxuries in Greece and Rome; cf. Soyer, *Pantropheion*, 137, 146, 154.

254. Aristophanes, *Frogs* 1503. The Greek is a trifle ambiguous in that it could also suggest that Timarion's friends and relations would mourn even more over his safe return since that would deprive them of their legacies. This cynical notion would fit the conventions of Byzantine satire as well as the characterisation of Theodore himself; cf. *Mazaris* 118.

255. On the various visions of hell, see Highet, *Anatomy of Satire,* 168–9. Compared to Lucian, the *Mazaris,* and Dante, the author's view is good-natured, and he is singularly uninterested in the torments of the damned; this one hurried allusion seems no more than a token genuflection towards such beliefs, no doubt another impiety in the eyes of Constantine Acropolites. It is an oddly assorted trio of victims. Alexander of Pherae was a noxious tyrant in 4th-century Greece, whom Dante, *Inf.* 12. 107, consigns to the Seventh Circle along with Dionysius I (tyrant of Syracuse in Sicily in the late 5th and 4th centuries), Attila the Hun, and a mismash of mythological monsters and real people, some of whom endure the same penalty of shovelling excrement. On Alexander's career, cf. Plutarch, *Pelopidas* 26–35. Nero, of course, was traditionally the Anti-Christ; the author's superlative (*kakiston*) term for his evil is equally standard. Quite why Philaretus is linked with these two is hard to say, since the author's sympathies for Romanus Diogenes should have made him approve the uprising of Philaretus in Armenia which Anna Comnena 6. 8–9 says was prompted by the blinding of that emperor. It may be that the author here wishes to reflect some official propaganda at the expense of sentiment and logic. Or it

may betoken his knowledge of that part of the world, since according to Boase, *The Cilician Kingdom of Armenia*, 3–4, "Cruelty and treachery characterised all Philaretus' acts and the Armenian chroniclers have little good to say of him." The other Greek source for Philaretus, who is not mentioned by Psellus, is the chronicler Zonaras 3. 692 Bonn (*PG* 135. 280). For such non-Greek sources as Michael the Syrian 15. 4 (transl. Chabot 3. 173), cf. Diehl, *Histoire du Moyen Age*, vol. 9, 517, putting Philaretus in the period 1072–86; see also Laurent, *REA* 9 (1929), 192–257. As to the shovelling of excrement, the manuscript has the singular participle *tarassonta*, thereby restricting it to Nero. Editors retain this, but Tode 34 alters it to the plural to include the other two.

256. Romano does not notice an echo here of Lucian, *Menippus or The Descent into Hell* 22, which also comes near the end of that dialogue.

257. Tozer, *JHS* 2 (1881), 256, thinks this contorted description indicates that chimneys were a novelty at the time. And indeed, according to Sprague de Camp, *The Ancient Engineers*, 357, they only start to appear in Europe in the 13th century. If so, Wilson 32 would be wrong in translating *kaminos* as chimney in an extract from the 9th-century chronicler Theophanes. But we have seen how the author becomes untypically strained in moments of *ecphrasis*, and that might be the reason for the present elaboration. One of his words, *orophiaios*, occurs elsewhere only in a single inscription, albeit Romano does not denote it as uncommon or late.

258. Thus effectively cutting Kydion off from any more interruptions.

259. Romano indicates the Greek *katharodiaitos*, also its following antonym *ryparodiaitos*, as late, giving no parallels. Stephanus' only entry for the first of these adjectives is an unverifiable allusion to Anastasius Sinaita; for the second, this passage only. Neither word is in *LSJ* or Lampe.

BIBLIOGRAPHY

EDITIONS OF THE *TIMARION*

HASE, M.   *Notices et extraits des manuscrits de la Bibliothèque impériale,* vol. 9, pt. 2 (Paris, 1813), 125–268.

ELLISSEN, A.   *Analekten der mittel- und neugriechischen Literatur,* vol. 4 (Leipzig, 1860), 1–185.

ROMANO, R.   *Timarione* (Naples, 1974).

The above are referred to by editor's name in the notes, as are:

TODE, H.   *De Timarione Dialogo Byzantino* (Diss. Greifswald, 1912).

WILSON, N. G.   *An Anthology of Byzantine Prose* (Berlin, 1971), 111–20, containing text with notes of chs. 3–10.

SECONDARY SOURCES

The following list registers the books and articles cited in the notes. For standard works of reference and editions of ancient authors, see below.

ALLBUTT, C.   *Greek Medicine in Rome* (London, 1921).

BALDWIN, B.   "Lucian and Europa: Variations on a Theme," *AC* 23 (1980), 115–20.

———.   "Priscus of Panium," *B* 50 (1980), 18–61.

———.   "Physical Descriptions of Byzantine Emperors," *B* 51 (1981), 8–21.

———.   "The Language and Style of Some Anonymous Byzantine Epigrams," *B* 52 (1982), 5–23.

———.   "A Talent to Amuse: Some Aspects of Byzantine Satire," *BF* 8 (1982), 19–28.

———.   "The Date and Purpose of the *Philopatris,*" *YCS* 27 (1982), 321–44.

BARKER, E.   *Social and Political Theory in Byzantium from Justinian to the Last Palaeologos* (Oxford, 1952).

Bibliography

BECK, H.-G.	*Kirche und theologische Literatur im byzantinischen Reich* (Munich, 1959).
———.	*Geschichte der byzantinischen Volksliteratur* (Munich, 1971).
BEHR, C. A.	*Aelius Aristides and the Sacred Tales* (Chicago, 1968).
BENJAMIN OF TUDELA.	*The Itinerary of Benjamin of Tudela,* ed. M. Adler (London, 1907).
BOASE, T. S. R.	*The Cilician Kingdom of Armenia* (Edinburgh, 1978).
BOWERSOCK, G. W.	*Greek Sophists in the Roman Empire* (Oxford, 1969).
BROWN, P.	*The Cult of the Saints* (Chicago, 1981).
BROWNING, R.	*Byzantium and Bulgaria* (London, 1975).
———.	"David Dishypatos' Poem on Akindynos," *B* 27 (1957), 713–45.
———.	"An Anonymous *basilikos logos* Addressed to Alexios I Comnenus," *B* 28 (1959), 31–50.
———.	"An Unnoticed Fragment of Sappho?" *CR* 10 (1960), 192–3.
———.	"The Death of John II Comnenus," *B* 31 (1961), 229–36.
———.	"A New Source on Byzantine-Hungarian Relations in the Twelfth Century," *Balkan Studies* 2 (1961), 173–214.
———.	"Unpublished Correspondence between Michael Italicus, Archbishop of Philippolis, and Theodore Prodromos," *Byzantino-bulgarica* 1 (1962), 279–97.
———.	"The Patriarchal School at Constantinople in the Twelfth Century," *B* 32 (1962), 167–201; 33 (1963), 11–40.
———.	"An Unpublished Corpus of Byzantine Poems," *B* 33 (1963), 289–316.
———.	"Enlightenment and Repression in Byzantium in the Eleventh and Twelfth Centuries," *PP* 69 (1975), 3–23.
———.	"The Language of Byzantine Literature," *Byzantina/Metabyzantina* 1 (1978), 105–33.
BUCKLER, G.	*Anna Comnena* (Oxford, 1929).
BURY, J. B.	*History of the Eastern Roman Empire* (London, 1912).

142

CAMERON, ALAN.   *Claudian: Poetry and Propaganda at the Court of Honorius* (Oxford, 1970).

———.   "Wandering Poets: A Literary Movement in Early Byzantine Egypt," *Historia* 14 (1965), 470–509.

CAMERON, AVERIL.   *Agathias* (Oxford, 1970).

CAMP, L. SPRAGUE DE   *The Ancient Engineers* (New York, 1974).

CASSON, L.   *Travel in the Ancient World* (Toronto, 1974).

CHALANDON, F.   *Les Comnène: Etudes sur l'empire byzantin au XIe et au XIIe siècles* (Paris, 1900–12).

CHEETHAM, N.   *Mediaeval Greece* (New Haven, 1981).

CHRIST, W., and PARANIKAS, M.   *Anthologia Graeca Carminum Christianorum* (Leipzig, 1871).

CLARKE, M. L.   *Brutus, the Noblest Roman* (London, 1981).

CLUCAS, L.   *The Trial of John Italus and the Crisis of Intellectual Values in the Eleventh Century* (Munich, 1981).

CODELLAS, P. S.   "The Case of Smallpox of Theodore Prodromos," *BHM* 20 (1946), 207–15.

CONSTANTELOS, D. J.   *Byzantine Philanthropy and Social Welfare* (New Brunswick, 1968).

CORMACK, R.   "The Classical Tradition in the Byzantine Provincial City: The Evidence of Thessalonica and Aphrodisias," in *Byzantium and the Classical Tradition,* ed. M. Mullett and R. Scott (Birmingham, 1981), 103–18.

CURTIUS, E.   *European Literature and the Latin Middle Ages* (English ed., New York, 1953).

DELEHAYE, H.   *Les légendes grecques des saints militaires* (Paris, 1909).

———.   "Constantini Acropolitae Hagiographi Byzantini Epistularum Manipulus," *AB* 51 (1933), 263–84.

DIEHL, C.   *Histoire du Moyen Age,* vol. 9, *L'Europe orientale de 1081 à 1453* (Paris, 1945).

———.   "Le légende de l'empereur Théophile," *Seminarium Kondakovium* 4 (1931), 37.

DIONISOTTI, A. C.   "From Ausonius' Schooldays? A Schoolbook and Its Relatives," *JRS* 72 (1982), 83–125.

DOWNEY, G.   "Nicolas Mesarites: Description of the

	Church of the Holy Apostles," *TAPhilS* 47. 6 (1957), 857–924.
DRÄSEKE, J.	"Michael Psellos im Timarion," *BZ* 6 (1897), 483–90.
———.	"Byzantinische Hadesfahrten," *NJKA* 29 (1912), 343–66.
DUDLEY, D. R.	*A History of Cynicism* (Cambridge, 1937).
DVORNIK, F.	*La vie de Saint Grégoire le Décapolite* (Paris, 1926).
EFTYCHIADIS, A.	"Curative Applications of the Types of Swings According to Byzantine Medicine," *Iatrologotechnike Stege* 13 (1981) (in Greek); English abstract in *SAMN* 9 (1982), 20.
FRIENDLY, A.	*The Dreadful Day* (London, 1981).
FUCHS, F.	*Die höheren Schulen von Konstantinopel im Mittelalter* (Leipzig, 1926).
GARZYA, A.	"Encomio inedito per Alessio Aristeno," *BF* 1 (1966), 92–114.
———.	"Precisazioni sul procèsso di Niceforo Basilace," *B* 40 (1970), 309–16.
———.	"Un lettre du milieu du XIIe siècle: Nicéphore Basilakès," *RESE* 8 (1970), 611–21.
———.	"Per la fortuna di Saffo a Bisanzio," *JOB* 20 (1971), 1–5.
———.	"Il *Pròlogo* di Niceforo Basilace," *Bollettino del comitato per la preparazione dell'Edizione Nazionale dei Classici Greci e Latini* 19 (1971), 55–71.
———.	"Literarische und rhetorische Polemiken der Komnenenzeit," *BS* 34 (1973), 1–14.
GOKEY, F. X.	*The Terminology for the Devil and Evil Spirits in the Apostolic Fathers* (Washington, D.C., 1961).
GRAINDOR, P.	*Un milliardaire antique: Hérode Atticus et sa famille* (Cairo, 1930).
GREPPIN, J.	"The Galenic Corpus in Classical Armenian: A Preliminary Report," *SAMN* 9 (1982), 11–13.
HALKIN, F.	"Distiques et notices propres au synaxaire de Chifflet," *AB* 66 (1948), 5–32.
———.	"Le synaxaire grec de Christ Church à Oxford," *AB* 66 (1948), 59–90.
———.	"Inscriptions grecques relatives à l'hagiographie," *AB* 70 (1952), 116–37.

HENDY, M.	*Coinage and Money in the Byzantine Empire* (Washington, D.C., 1969).
HESSELING, D. C., and PERNOT, L.	*Poèmes Prodromiques en grec vulgaire* (Amsterdam, 1910).
HIGHET, G.	*Anatomy of Satire* (Princeton, 1962).
HORNA, K.	*Einige unedierte Stucke des Manasses und Italikos* (Vienna, 1902).
———.	"Das Hodoiporikon des Konstantin Manasses," *BZ* 13 (1904), 313–55.
HOUSEHOLDER, F. W.	"Mock Decrees in Lucian," *TAPA* 71 (1944), 199–216.
HUNGER, H.	*Die hochsprachliche profane Literatur der Byzantiner* (Munich, 1978).
———.	*Der byzantinische Katz-Mause-Krieg* (Graz, 1968).
———.	"Anonymes Pamphlet gegen eine byzantinische Mafia," *RESE* 7 (1969), 95–107.
———.	"On the Imitation (Mimesis) of Antiquity in Byzantine Literature," *DOP* 23–24 (1969–70), 15–38.
HUSSEY, J. M.	*Church and Learning in the Byzantine Empire 867–1185* (Cambridge, 1937).
JEFFREYS, M.	"The Nature and Origins of the Political Verse," *DOP* 28 (1974), 143–95.
KANTOROWICZ, E.	"Oriens Augusti—Lever du Roi," *DOP* 17 (1963), 117–77.
KARLSSON, G.	*Idéologie et cérémonial dans l'epistographie byzantine* (Uppsala, 1959).
KAZHDAN, A. P.	"Some Questions Addressed to the Scholars Who Believe in the Authenticity of Kaminiates' 'Capture of Thessalonica,' " *BZ* 71 (1978), 301–14.
KENNEDY, G.	*Classical Rhetoric and Its Christian and Secular Tradition from Ancient to Modern Times* (Chapel Hill, 1980).
KIRCHNER, J.	*Prosopographia Attica* (repr. Berlin, 1966).
KIRK, G. S., and RAVEN, J. E.	*The PreSocratic Philosophers* (Cambridge, 1960).
KRUMBACHER, K.	*Geschichte der byzantinischen Litteratur* (2nd ed., Munich, 1897).
KURZ, E.	"Unedierte Texte aus der Zeit des Kaisers John Komnenos," *BZ* 16 (1907), 69–119.

Bibliography

KUSTAS, G.	*Studies in Byzantine Rhetoric* (Thessalonica, 1973).
KYRIAKIS, M.	"Satire and Slapstick in Seventh and Twelfth Century Byzantium," *Byzantina* 5 (1973), 291–306.
———.	"Of Professors and Disciples in Twelfth Century Byzantium," *B* 43 (1973), 108–19.
———.	"Poor Poets and Starving Literati in Twelfth Century Byzantium," *B* 44 (1974), 290–309.
LABAGE, M.	*Medieval Travellers: The Rich and Restless* (London, 1983).
LAIOU-THOMA-DAKIS, A. E.	*Peasant Society in the Late Byzantine Empire* (Princeton, 1977).
———.	"The Byzantine Economy in the Mediterranean Trade Systems," *DOP* 34–35 (1980–1), 177–222.
LAMMA, P.	*Comneni e Staufer,* vol. 1 (Rome, 1955).
LATTIMORE, R.	*Themes in Greek and Latin Epitaphs* (Urbana, 1962).
LAURENT, J.	"Byzance et Antioche sous le curopalate Philarète," *REA* 9 (1929), 61–72.
———.	"Le Duc d'Antioche Khatchatour 1068–1072," *BZ* 30 (1929–30), 405–11.
LEMERLE, P.	"Saint Démétrius de Thessalonique," *BCH* 77 (1953), 660–94.
———.	"La composition et la chronologie des deux premiers livres des Miracula S. Demetrii," *BZ* 46 (1953), 349–61.
LEONE, P.	"Nicephori Gregorae Oratio in regem Cypri," *B* 51 (1981), 211–24.
LITTLEWOOD, A. R.	"Romantic Paradise: The Role of the Garden in Byzantine Romance," *BMGS* 5 (1979), 95–114.
MAAS, P.	"Die Musen der Kaisers Alexius I," *BZ* 22 (1913), 348–62.
MACCORMACK, S.	*Art and Ceremony in Late Antiquity* (Berkeley, 1981).
MACLEOD, M. D.	Review of Romano's *Timarione, JHS* 96 (1976), 271.
MAGOULIAS, H. J.	"The Lives of the Saints as Sources of Data for the History of Byzantine Medicine in the 6th and 7th Centuries," *BZ* 57 (1964), 127–50.

MAGUIRE, H. *Art and Eloquence in Byzantium* (Princeton, 1981).

MANGO, C. *Byzantium: The Empire of New Rome* (London, 1980).

———. "Byzantine Literature as a Distorting Mirror," *PP* 80 (1975), 3–18.

———. "Discontinuity with the Classical Past," in *Byzantium and the Classical Tradition*, ed. M. Mullett and R. Scott (Birmingham, 1981), 48–60.

MATHIEU, M. "Une source négligée de la bataille de Mantzikert," *B* 20 (1950), 89–103.

MAZARIS. *Mazaris' Journey to Hades*, ed. J. N. Barry, M. J. Share, A. Smithies, and L. G. Westerink (Buffalo, 1975).

MEYENDORFF, J. *Byzantine Theology* (New York, 1974).

MOFFATT, A. "Schooling in the Iconoclast Centuries," in *Iconoclasm*, ed. A. A. Bryer and J. Herrin (Birmingham, 1977), 85–92.

MORRIS, R. "The Powerful and the Poor in Tenth-Century Byzantium: Law and Reality," *PP* 73 (1976), 3–27.

MULLETT, M. "The Classical Tradition in the Byzantine Letter," in *Byzantium and the Classical Tradition*, ed. M. Mullett and R. Scott (Birmingham, 1981), 75–93.

NICOL, D. M. "Constantine Akropolites: A Prosopographical Note," *DOP* 19 (1965), 249–56.

OESTRICH, G. "Die Antike Literatur als Vorbild der praktischen Wissenschaften im 16 und 17 Jahrundert," in *Classical Influences on European Culture 1500–1700*, ed. R. Bolgar (Cambridge, 1974), 315–24.

OSTROGORSKY, G. *History of the Byzantine State* (English ed., Oxford, 1968).

PAPADEME-TRIOU, J. T. "*Ta Schede tou myos:* New Sources and Texts," in *Classical Studies Presented to Ben Edwin Perry* (Urbana, 1969), 210–22.

PAPADEME-TRIOU, S. D. *Fedor Prodromos: Istoriko-literaturnoe izsledovanie* [Theodore Prodromos: Historical and literary studies] (Odessa, 1905).

PAPAGEORGIU, P. N. "Zu Manasses und Italikos," *BZ* 12 (1903), 258–60.

Bibliography

PAPE, W., and BENSELER, G.	*Griechische Eigennamen* (repr. Graz, 1959).
PFEIFFER, R.	*History of Classical Scholarship* (Oxford, 1968).
PHILIPS, E. D.	*Greek Medicine* (London, 1973).
PODESTA, G.	"Le satire Lucianesche di Teodoro Prodromo," *Aevum* 19 (1945), 239–52; 21 (1947), 3–25.
POLEMIS, D. I.	*The Doukai: A Contribution to Byzantine Prosopography* (London, 1968).
POLIAKOVA, S., TELENKOV, I., and LIPSIC, J.	"Vizantijskaia satira Timarion" [The Byzantine satire *Timarion*], *VVrem* 6 (1953), 357–65.
ROMANO, R.	*Nicola Callicle Carmi* (Naples, 1980).
———.	"Sulla possibile attribuzione del *Timarione* pseudo-Lucianeo a Nicola Callicle," *GIF* 25 (1973), 309–15.
———.	"Sulla poesia di Nicola Callicle," *Annali di Facoltà di Lettere e Filosophia Università Napoli* 22 (1979–80), 61–75.
RUNCIMAN, S.	*The Medieval Manichee* (Oxford, 1947).
———.	*A History of the Crusades,* vol. 2 (Cambridge, 1952).
———.	*The Eastern Schism* (Oxford, 1955).
———.	*Byzantine Style and Civilization* (London, 1975).
SARTON, G.	*Galen of Pergamum* (Lawrence, Kansas, 1954).
SCARBOROUGH, J.	*Roman Medicine* (London, 1969).
SCHMITT, W.	"Cato im Byzance," *Klio* 48 (1967), 325–34.
SHARF, A.	*Byzantine Jewry from Justinian to the Fourth Crusade* (London, 1971).
SHEPARD, J.	"Tzetzes' Letters to Leo at Distra," *BF* 6 (1979), 191–240.
SIMON, B.	"Black Bile and Melancholia: Some Fantasies about Facts," *SAMN* 6 (1980), 3–4.
SINKEWICZ, R. E.	"A Fragment of Barlaam's Work 'On the Gods Introduced by the Greeks,' " *Byz. St.* 9. 2 (1982), 211–19.
SNIPES, K.	"A Letter of Michael Psellos to Constantine, Nephew of the Patriarch Cerularius," *GRBS* 22 (1981), 89–107.
SOYER, A.	*The Pantropheon* (repr. London, 1977).

STERNBACH, L.   "Nicolai Calliclis carmina," *Rozprawy Akademii Umiejetnosci, Widzial Filologiczny* 21 (1903), 315–92.

———.   "Ein Schmähgedicht des Michael Psellos," *WS* 25 (1903), 10–39.

STILWELL, R.   *Antioch on the Orontes*, vol. 2, *The Excavations, 1933–36* (Princeton, 1938).

TEMKIN, O.   *Galenism: Rise and Decline of a Medical Philosophy* (Ithaca, 1973).

———.   "Byzantine Medicine," *DOP* 16 (1962), 97–115.

THEODOROS PRODROMOS.   *Theodoros Prodromos: Historische Gedichte*, ed. W. Hörandner (Vienna, 1974).

THUMB, A.   "Die griechischen Lehnwörter im Armenischen," *BZ* 9 (1900), 388–452.

TOVAR, A.   "Nicetas of Heraclea and Byzantine Grammatical Doctrine," in *Classical Studies Presented to Ben Edwin Perry* (Urbana, 1969), 223–35.

TOZER, H. F.   "Byzantine Satire," *JHS* 2 (1881), 233–70.

TREADGOLD, W.   *The Nature of the Bibliotheca of Photius* (Washington, D.C., 1980).

TREU, M.   "Ein Kritiker des Timarion," *BZ* 1 (1892), 361–5.

TRYPANIS, C.   *The Penguin Book of Greek Verse* (London, 1971).

USPENSKIJ, F.   "Deloproivodsto po obvineniju Ioanna Itala v eresi" [Records of the trial of John Italus for heresy], *IRAIC* 2 (1897), 1–66.

VASILIEV, A. A.   *History of the Byzantine Empire* (Madison, 1964).

VICKERS, M.   "Sirmium or Thessalonica?" *BZ* 67 (1974), 337–50.

VYRONIS, S.   "The *Panegyris* of the Byzantine Saint: A Study in the Nature of a Medieval Institution, Its Origins and Fate," in *The Byzantine Saint*, ed. S. Hackel (Birmingham, 1981), 196–228.

WALZ, C.   *Rhetores Graeci* (Tübingen, 1832–6).

———.   *Anecdota Byzantina* (Diss. Leipzig, 1910).

WALZER, R.   *Galen on Jews and Christians* (Oxford, 1949).

WEBER, T., and KODER, J.   *Liutprand von Cremona in Konstantinopel* (Vienna, 1980).

149

WEST, M. L.	"Near Eastern Materials in Hellenistic and Roman Literature," *HSCP* 73 (1969), 113–34.
WILSON, N. G.	"Books and Readers in Byzantium," in *Byzantine Books and Bookmen* (Washington, D.C., 1975), 1–15.

A NOTE ON PRIMARY SOURCES AND FURTHER READING

Up to a point, the *Timarion* can be enjoyed by itself. But works of literature rarely exist in a vacuum, certainly not satire. Some further acquaintance with the historical background and the literary genre will sharpen the reader's appreciation of both general and particular points.

The student of the *Timarion* is doubly fortunate: two of the (by common consent) greatest works of Byzantine literature are directly relevant, and both are available in English translation. These are, of course, the *Chronographia* of Michael Psellus and the *Alexiad* of Anna Comnena. I elsewhere (note 224) provide a general sketch of Psellus' career and writings. His *Chronographia* was edited by C. Sathas (London, 1899; repr. New York, 1979), and by E. Renauld in the Budé series (Paris, 1926–8; repr. 1967). There is an English translation under the title *Fourteen Byzantine Rulers* by E. R. A. Sewter in the Penguin Classics series (London, 1966). The section on Romanus IV Diogenes in Book Seven will be of particular interest to readers of the *Timarion*.

In a work of filial piety, Anna Comnena covers the period 1069–1118, the lifetime of her father, who became the emperor Alexius I in 1081. The title *Alexiad* is meant to remind her readers of such epic classics as the *Iliad* and the *Aeneid*. For readers of the *Timarion,* her most evident interest is in what she has to say about Romanus Diogenes, John Italus, Nicolas Callicles, Psellus, and Philaretus. But the overall picture of the early Comnenan period she provides is just as valuable for appreciating the Byzantium of our satire's author. The *Alexiad* was edited in the Budé series by B. Leib (3 vols.,

Paris, 1937–45; P. Gautier added an index volume in 1976). There are two English versions, respectively by E. Dawes (London, 1928) and Sewter in the Penguin series (1969).

One of the several sources for the eleventh century is Anna's own husband, the caesar Nicephorus Bryennius. This marital team of historiographers may smack slightly of the late Will and Ariel Durant. A French version of Bryennius is provided by H. Grégoire, *B* 23 (1953), 469–530; 25–27 (1955–57), 881–926. Grégoire also provides the same service for part of the history by Michael Attaleiates, *B* 28 (1958), 325–62. Also relevant to the *Timarion* for what they have to say about the period of Romanus Diogenes are the chronicles of John Scylitzes and John Zonaras. There are no English versions of these writers, whose texts are edited both in the Bonn *Corpus Scriptorum Historiae Byzantinae* (1828–97—currently in the process of revision and amplification) and in *PG*. As my notes disclose, there are some interesting discrepancies between these writers, Psellus, and the *Timarion*.

For the period after Anna Comnena, we are fortunate in having the accounts of John Cinnamus and Nicetas Choniates, and are again doubly blessed by English translations: Cinnamus is translated by C. M. Brand under the title *Deeds of John and Manuel Comnenus* (New York, 1976), whilst Harry Magoulias has recently provided a version of Choniates, to be published by Wayne State University Press.

Along with the author of the *Timarion*, two of the liveliest literary pens in the twelfth century were wielded by Theodore Prodromos and John Tzetzes. Prodromos is of particular interest here, not only as a satirist in his own right, but as a possible character and possible author of the *Timarion*. For these reasons, my Introduction and Notes abound with references to him. Extracts from his satirical works can be found in the articles by Kyriakis listed in the Bibliography, also (if they are his—it is a matter of continuing controversy) from the so-called Beggar Poems in Trypanis' *Penguin Book of Greek Verse*. As for Tzetzes, there are some extensive extracts along with illuminating discussion in the article listed above by M. Jeffreys. For the intellectual life of the period, including some mention of the *Timarion* and its characters, Hussey's *Church and Learning* remains one of the most useful.

As has been made abundantly clear, the *Timarion* is not unique. A later work, *Mazaris,* composed in the fifteenth century in the reign of Manuel II, also has a protagonist who goes down to Hades before his time and has various encounters before his return to life. There are some similarities of detail, also some very basic differences of tone and treatment. Thanks to the English version accompanying the edition mentioned in the Bibliography, the two pieces may be compared and contrasted by all readers.

Somewhat closer to the *Timarion* in language and tone, albeit not involving a descent into Hades, is the *Philopatris (Patriot)*, a work of quite uncertain date (cf. my article in *YCS* 27) but fairly to be reckoned as Byzantine. There is an English translation in volume 8 of the Loeb edition/translation of Lucian, by M. D. Macleod.

Lucian himself, the Syrian-born Greek satirist of the second century A.D., is the prime literary model of the *Timarion*, as countless references in the notes of myself and Romano attest. Although stigmatised by some Byzantines as the Anti-Christ (a label he deserves no more than that of "the Voltaire of antiquity" bestowed upon him by Macaulay), he remained a much admired and much imitated stylist. As Professor Robert Browning (in a letter of March 2, 1983) mentioned to me, the number of references to him in Byzantine manuals of rhetoric suggests that some of his works were used as classroom exemplars. In the present context, it is worth emphasising that a fair number of these references (in Walz, *Rhetores Graeci* 2. 53, 497, 512, 637; 3. 521, 526; 5. 573; 7. 1138) are to the *Cataplus (Downward Journey)*. This along with the *Menippus or Descent into Hell* are the two works of Lucian most thematically relevant to the *Timarion*. Other pieces well worth the reader's attention in this regard are *Charon or The Inspectors, Icaromenippus (The Skyman)*, *Lover of Lies,* and the *Dialogues of the Dead.* All are accessible in the Loeb edition of Lucian, translated by A. H. Harmon, K. Kilburn, and Macleod.

INDEX

Acherusian Lake, 18, 51, 103 n. 105
Achilles Tatius, 95 n. 66
Aeacus, 51, 52, 54, 60, 64
Aelian, 107 n. 125
Aelius Aristides, 74, 116 n. 168, 137 n. 248
Aeneas, 47
Aeschylus, 122 n. 188
Aesculapius: god of healing, 51, 52, 60, 61, 66, 69, 71, 116 n. 168; remedies of, 137 n. 248; veil of, 67
Aesop, 10
Agathias, 132 n. 234
Akindynos (anti-Hesychast poet), 124 n. 201
Albertus Magnus: compared with Psellus, 128 n. 224
Alcibiades: his lisp ridiculed, 128 n. 224
Alexander (emperor, 912): pig-like life of, 134 n. 243
Alexander of Pherae: career and cruelty of, 138 n. 255; in Hell, 75
Alexander the Great: bravery of, 125 n. 206; Diogenes and, 73, 130 n. 230; enslaves Asia, 83 n. 16
Alexius I: compared to Sun, 136 n. 247; defeats Petchenegs, 84 n. 20; his poem to his son, 103 n. 104; issues coins to honour St Demetrius, 86 n. 24; and John Italus, 131 n. 232; and the *Timarion*, 30–31, 36
Alexius Macrembolites, 8, 27
Ammianus Marcellinus, 93 n. 58
Anastasius (emperor): satirised, 11
Anastasius Sinaita, 139 n. 259
Anaxagoras, 72, 130 n. 230
Anaximenes, 130 n. 230
Andronicus II, 26
Andronicus (son of Manuel II), 85 n. 23
Anna Comnena, 82 n. 12, 83 n. 16, 87 n. 28, 95 n. 64, 108 n. 129, 119 n. 179, 133 n. 238; historical work of, 150–51

—*Alexiad* 1. 1, 35; 1. 6, 129 n. 229; 1. 7, 87 n. 28; 1. 8, 128 n. 224; 2. 6, 94 n. 61; 3. 3, 30, 87 n. 27; 5. 8, 131 n. 232; 5. 9, 30, 31, 131 n. 232; 6. 7, 31; 6. 8, 138 n. 255; 7. 11, 129 n. 229; 9. 8, 94 n. 61; 10. 2, 94 n. 61; 12. 2, 94 n. 61; 12. 4, 84 n. 22; 12. 5, 94 n. 61; 13. 4, 94 n. 61; 13. 10, 96 n. 72; 14. 9, 94 n. 61; 15. 2, 82 n. 8; 15. 6, 108 n. 129, 109 n. 135; 15. 7, 91 n. 45, 98 n. 85
Anna Ducaena, 96 n. 68
Antiochus, 61, 116 n. 172
Antony, Mark, 36
Aphrodite, 48
Apocalypse of Esdras, 115 n. 162
Appian, 117 n. 172
Arab: headdresses, 64, 67; horses, 46; sack of Thessalonica, 85 n. 23, 125 n. 205
Archelaus (medical writer), 99 n. 87
Archilochus, 133 n. 235
Arctos (Great Bear), 75
Ares, 46, 48; compared with Dawn, 92 n. 53
Arethas, 12, 135 n. 244
Aristarchus, 71, 127 n. 223
Aristides (Church Father), 116 n. 168
Aristides the Just, 119 n. 179
Aristophanes: *Acharnians*, 134 n. 243; fr. 51, 88 n. 32; *Frogs* 1503, 138 n. 254; on food, 110 n. 138; and the *Timarion*, 8, 133 n. 234; *Wasps* 721, 126 n. 213
—*Clouds* 1367, 126 n. 213; 1397, 82 n. 7
Aristotle: appealed to by John Italus, 74; in Byzantium and the West, 134 n. 242; commentary on by Theodore of Smyrna, 113 n. 149; in Dante, 117 n. 173; rhetorical theories of, 136 n. 246
—*Nic. Eth.* 1129b28, 96 n. 71; 1145a29, 97 n. 79
Armenia, 75, 111 n. 140, 121 n. 187
Asia: Christianity in, 62; enslaved by Alexander, 83 n. 16

65; 4. 230, 97 n. 74; 6. 230, 92 n. 54; 7.
157, 95 n. 65; 9. 39, 81 n. 7; 16. 23, 81
n. 3; 17. 41, 81 n. 3; 23. 157, 92 n. 54;
24. 20, 109 n. 133; 24. 51, 95 n. 65
Hunting, 15, 43, 87 n. 27

Iberians, 44, 90 n. 40
Iconoclasm, 21, 118–19 n. 179
Ionic accent, 61, 116 n. 169
Isaeus: on funerals, 126 n. 216
Isidore (patriarch), 27
Italy, 15, 44, 47, 90 n. 40; Italian dresses,
122 n. 187

Jews: aversion to pork, 43; Byzantine
hostility to, 15, 86–87 n. 26, 134 n. 243
John, son of Manuel II, 12
John Damascene, 116 n. 168
John Italus: career and trial of, 131–32 n.
232; consul of the philosophers, 112 n.
147, 113 n. 149; fights with Diogenes,
23, 73–74; his philosophy and rhetoric,
135–36 n. 245; relationship to *Timarion,* 30–31; unpopular in Hell, 72
John Lydus, 11, 114 n. 153
John Mauropous: connection with Psellus, 128 n. 224; Paphlagonian origins
of, 135 n. 244
John of Ephesus, 12
John Philoponus: on Galen, 118 n. 173;
Photius on, 12
John Pikatoros, 8
John II Comnenus: connection with *Timarion,* 31, 36; defeats Petchenegs, 84
n. 20; exiles Michael Palaeologus Ducas, 94 n. 63; murder of, 22, 120 n.
183; speech to by Michael Italicus, 36,
132 n. 234
John the Logothete: commentaries on
Hermogenes, 136 n. 246
Julian the Apostate: abused by Byzantines, 12; on Christians, 21; possible influence on *Timarion,* 104 n. 107, 107 n.
126
Julius Caesar, 95 n. 67, 133 n. 239;
murder of, 22, 63, 120 n. 183
Justice, 21; Byzantine corruption of, 115

n. 164; courtroom procedure, 121 n.
186, 129 nn. 227, 228; in Hades, 120–
21 n. 183; *Timarion* on, 60, 64
Justinian I: in Dante, 119 n. 179; headgear of, 122 n. 187; persecution of
heretics by, 131 n. 232, 133 n. 234; re-
moves prostitutes from streets, 10; and
Theodora, 30
Juvenal: satiric themes of, 10, 107 n. 125

Kydion, 13–15, 24, 41, 42, 43, 44, 45, 46,
49, 50, 53, 74, 76, 81 n. 3, 82 n. 10, 83
n. 19, 105 n. 111, 105 n. 115, 139 n.
258

Leo III: law code of, 108 n. 130
Leo VI: his poem on Hell, 98 n. 81, 104
n. 106
Lethe, 110 n. 138
Libanius, 128 n. 224
Lichudes, 128 n. 224
Liutprand of Cremona: on Byzantine eating habits, 106 n. 118; on Byzantine
ethnic insults, 90 n. 41
Lodgings: in Hades, 19, 53; at Hebrus,
18, 50; in Thessalonica, 14, 49
Longinus, 136 n. 246
Lucian: connection with *Timarion,* 1–2;
model for Byzantine satire, 8–13, 34–
35; possible influence on *Timarion,* 82
n. 10, 98 n. 81, 102 n. 96, 104 n. 110,
115 n. 161, 116 n. 169, 118 n. 173, 123
n. 193, 125 n. 207, 129 n. 226, 130 n.
231, 138 n. 255; selected works of, 152.
Works: *Affairs of the Heart,* 104 n. 108;
Alexander, 97 n. 75, 135 n. 244;
Charon, 90 n. 42; *Cock,* 107 n. 125,
114 n. 152, 114 n. 156; *Council of the
Gods,* 132 n. 233; *Demonax,* 96 n. 70;
Dialogues of the Dead, 35, 103 n. 102;
Downward Journey, 114 n. 156;
Dream, 103 n. 100; *Fake Sophist,* 133
n. 235; *Grief,* 105 n. 112; *Hermotimus,*
91 n. 43, 92 n. 53; *Icaromenippus,* 129
n. 229; *Imagines,* 91 n. 49; *Lexiphanes,*
81 n. 1, 123 n. 195, 124 n. 203; *Long-
Lived,* 35; *Lover of Lies,* 83 n. 18, 101

157

Index